HENRY FRANCIS LYTE

HENRY FRANCIS LYTE

Brixham's Poet and Priest

by

B. G. SKINNER

Vicar of Brixham

UNIVERSITY OF EXETER

1974

ISBN 0 900771 92 5

Printed in England by James Townsend & Sons Limited Exeter
and Published by the University of Exeter

CONTENTS

PREFACE

TO THOSE who know something of the immensely fascinating life of the author of 'Abide with Me', it must seem strange that no comprehensive or definitive biography of him has ever been published. Three years after the poet's death his daughter, Mrs A. M. M. Hogg, wrote the *Remains of the late Henry Francis Lyte, MA,* published by F. & J. Rivington in 1850. This included a selection of Lyte's poems, hymns and sermons with extracts from some of his letters and a fifty-six page Prefatory Memoir by the authoress. The latter is the daughter's pen-picture of a father she deeply admired and loved and gives some useful first-hand information about certain events in Lyte's life. It is, however, in no sense a thoroughgoing biography.

The next work of any size on Lyte's life did not appear until 1939 when the Rev. John Appleyard, Congregational Minister of Brixham from 1896–1908 and from 1917–42, wrote *Henry Francis Lyte,* published by the Epworth Press. This is a brief work of less than 15,000 words and could not claim to give more than a sketch of the poet's life.

It so happened that Lyte's great-grandson, the late Walter Maxwell-Lyte, whose father was Sir Henry Maxwell-Lyte, Deputy Keeper of the Public Records, planned to publish a definitive biography of his ancestor on the occasion of the centenary of H. F. Lyte's death in 1947. He did a fair amount of research on the subject, which we have acknowledged where applicable in the text and footnotes, and actually wrote a Preface, an opening chapter entitled 'Ancestry and Parentage' and a few more typescript sheets covering Lyte's life up to about 1816.

At the same time, however, the Rev. H. J. Garland was also preparing a book on Lyte, but he did not consult Walter Maxwell-Lyte or the Lyte family until his manuscript was nearly completed. As Garland died in 1951 the appearance of his book was delayed, and it was not until 1956 that it was eventually published, under the editorship of Leonard Melling, by the Torch Publishing Company, Manchester. Its title was *Henry Francis Lyte and the Story of Abide with Me.*

Walter Maxwell-Lyte, a Ministry of Food official still at work at sixty-seven years of age in 1947, was somewhat discouraged by this threat to forestall him. Although as late as 1951 he still hoped to publish his book he never finally did so, being by this time somewhat handicapped by advancing age. This was in some ways unfortunate, as Maxwell-Lyte had taken much more trouble than Garland to verify his facts.

Garland was an elderly Methodist minister who had been appointed to the Newton Abbot Methodist Circuit in Edward VII's reign, some fifty years before his book was published. He remained in the area for ten years, during which time he befriended Lyte's grand-daughter Miss A. M. M. Hogg of Berry Head. She gave him every assistance in his researches on Lyte and seems to have shown him more of the family letters and papers than any other biographer of Lyte has seen, apart from Mrs Hogg. Thus Garland can write in an almost matter-of-fact way about Mr Barlow and his daughter Julia, or John Patterson (the priest who after death appeared to Lyte in a vision) when even Walter Maxwell-Lyte could not discover anything about them. We can only suppose that the relevant correspondence which Garland saw about 1907 had disappeared by 1947. There are several valuable quotations from the Lyte family's letters in Garland's book, which as far as we know cannot be seen elsewhere. Garland had the great advantage, too, of being able in 1907 to speak to a number of people who could still remember Lyte from personal acquaintance. So his book contains a good deal of useful material.

On the other hand only about fifty of Garland's 196 pages deal with Lyte's life; most of his book is taken up with replies received to a circular letter he sent to a wide variety of people asking for stories and experiences involving the hymn 'Abide with Me'. Garland's editor admits, on page 195, that there is a deficiency of biographical material and calls the first part of the book a 'biographical sketch' of Lyte. After his ten years in Torbay area Garland lived for the rest of his life far away from Devon; at the time of writing the book he was serving first at Millom, Cumberland and then at Ramsgate. There is every sign, in fact, that his book was compiled rather hastily from notes made many years before. Much as Garland's work is still valued by admirers of Lyte in Brixham and Torbay, it cannot be said to provide the definitive biography which Walter Maxwell-Lyte was so anxious to write.

Through the kindness of Walter Maxwell-Lyte's son, Mr Jack W. Maxwell-Lyte of Epsom, and his kinsman Mr B. E. N. Lyte of Caythorpe, Lincs., the author has been given access to all the Lyte family papers still surviving. Valuable as these papers are, they only constitute a small part of the writings which Lyte left at his death. A letter from Walter Maxwell-

Lyte to the then Headmaster of Portora written on 23 July 1951, states 'Unfortunately most of his papers and diaries were destroyed after his death'. The *Remains,* page lix, says: 'Among our author's MSS was found a note strongly expressive of his desire that no journals which he had left undestroyed should ever be made public, regarding any idea of possible publicity attached to such records as depriving them of their strictly private and sacred character. This prohibition does not, we conceive, extend to his letters'. Garland and Appleyard did not quote from the diaries, though they made use of some facts contained in them. In December 1946, however, Walter Maxwell-Lyte wrote in a letter to the Headmaster of Portora: 'I think that after 100 years some discretion might be exercised (sc. with regard to publishing Lyte's private papers)', and it is in this spirit that we have quoted from them.

The present Headmaster of Portora, the Rev. P. H. Rogers, kindly lent us the school's file on H. F. Lyte, which includes various letters written by Walter Maxwell-Lyte about 1947 to the then Headmaster, the Rev. D. L. Graham, discussing details of Lyte's history. One or two Lyte family letters which now seem to have disappeared are quoted in this correspondence.

Other sources include the Crediton testimonials, a photo-copy of the Julia letter and other material kindly lent by Mr J. A. Palmes of Chagford, a great-grandson of Lyte, who sadly died in January 1972 in the midst of our correspondence. The Exeter Diocesan Registrar and the Devon County Archivist have given us access to many church documents. Material concerning Lyte's ordination and ministry in Ireland has kindly been sent by Canon J. S. Brown, Warden of the Divinity Hostel, Trinity College, Dublin; Miss G. Willis of the Representative Church Body Library, Dublin; the Rev. R. W. Neill, St Canice's Library, Kilkenny and the Rev. E. Brandon, Rector of Foulksmills and Taghmon. Local material has been furnished by the Torbay County Borough Librarian, Mr J. R. Pike, and his colleagues at the Torquay, Paignton and Brixham Libraries, also by the Exeter and Plymouth City Libraries, the Exeter Cathedral Library, Exeter University Library and the Devon and Exeter Institution Library. Local newspapers have been consulted in the British Museum Newspaper Library, Colindale. We are most grateful to the staff of all these institutions for their kind help.

It has not been easy to obtain adequate material on the long period Lyte spent in Brixham. Lyte is a legendary figure in the town and the fund of stories told about him is considerable, but evidence in black and white is hard to obtain. One reason for this is that the busy seafarers of nineteenth-century Brixham had neither the time nor the inclination to write about the town and its people. The author has nevertheless made the fullest possible enquiries, through the local press, from Mr J. Horsley and Mr C. H. Rock (two successive Hon. Curators of Brixham Museum), from Mr W. A. Saxton (a local historian and formerly Clerk to Brixham Urban District Council) and all other promising sources. The owners of Lytes Cary Manor; Nevada House, Marazion; Sway Place; Bramble Tor, Dittisham; Berry Head House and 'Whitegates' (formerly Burton House), Brixham and Dartington Parsonage have been most helpful in showing the author over these houses and we greatly appreciate the kind co-operation given.

This is a shortened version of a thesis which was accepted by the University of Exeter in 1973 for the MA degree. The author wishes to express his thanks to Professor J. R. Porter, MA for his kind help in preparing the manuscript for publication; to his Supervisor Canon J. A. Thurmer, MA for his continued help and encouragement; to the University Publications Committee and their Chairman Professor W. L. D. Ravenhill, MA PhD, for their kind assistance in arranging for the work to be published.

B. G. SKINNER.

Brixham.
December 1973.

THE CRADLE OF HENRY FRANCIS LYTE

THE HISTORY of some of the greatest English families shows the re-appearance of brilliance after generations of relative obscurity. This is true of the Churchills and the Cecils and it is certainly true of the Lytes. Two miles from their parish church of Charlton Mackrell in Somerset stands Lytes Cary Manor, the family's ancient home. A trifle small for a country mansion, it is none the less a delightful and venerable old building. The earliest part is the fourteenth-century chapel, and the fifteenth-century hall is adorned with one of the finest collections of family armorials in stained glass to be seen in this land.

Peter le Lyt, who died in 1348, was probably the first to live at Lytes Cary but as early as 1255 his grandfather William le Lyt, Sergeant-at-Law in Edward I's reign, lived nearby.[1] The name Lyt in Middle English meant 'little', such as Short or Brown or any such name. A direct descendant of William was the famous Elizabethan botanist Henry Lyte (1529–1607) whose translation from the Flemish of Dodoens' *Herbal*, with 870 woodcuts and many notes by Lyte himself, obtained wide popularity. Known as *Lyte's Herbal* it ran into five editions between 1586 and 1678. Even more noted was Henry's son Thomas Lyte the genealogist, who was born about 1568 and succeeded to Lytes Cary in 1607. So impressed was King James I by Lyte's splendid genealogical table 'Brittans Monarchie', which traced James' ancestry back to Brutus, that he presented Lyte with a miniature of the King by Hilliard studded with diamonds, the well-known 'Lyte Jewel' now in the British Museum. Thomas Lyte drew up two pedigrees of his own family showing his father Henry Lyte to have been the eleventh in direct succession from William le Lyt. Later work[2] shows our H. F. Lyte to have been the ninth in direct descent from Henry. Another distinguished Lyte was the genealogist's half-brother Henry (born 1573) who appears to have pioneered the use of decimals in Britain, though his book *The Art of*

[1] H. C. Maxwell-Lyte, *Proceedings of the Somerset Archaeological and Natural History Society*, 1892, Part II, pp. 1f.
[2] H. C. Maxwell-Lyte, *loc. cit.*

Tens and Decimal Arithmetike (published 1619) seems to have borrowed freely from a French work, *La Disme,* published in 1590.[1]

In 1740 another Thomas Lyte, great-grandson of the genealogist, unfortunately had to convey part of the house to trustees so that the rents might be used to discharge his debts. In 1748 he transferred the estate to his son John, who mortgaged it to Francis Fane who in his turn sold it to Thomas Lockyer of Ilchester. Not only had the house passed from the Lytes but it soon fell into a bad state of neglect, and it is fortunate that the Manor was purchased in 1907 by Sir Walter Jenner, Bt. (son of the famous Victorian physician Sir William Jenner) who beautifully restored it and bequeathed it to its present owners The National Trust.

The above John Lyte after mortgaging the house moved to nearby Pilton and then to Bath. His second son was Captain Thomas Lyte, born at Bath in January 1766 and destined to be the father of Henry Francis Lyte. Captain Lyte's autobiography, an extraordinary document filling 105 pages of an exercise book, was written 'to show my children and descendants the follies into which both my ancestors and myself have fallen, which I hope will act as a caution to them to be more circumspect and prudent and to avoid those difficulties, which want of thought (not to give it a more severe epithet) has involved the Family of Lyte.' The account is so utterly frank, and in one sense damaging to Captain Lyte himself, that the reader may wonder if the author was revelling in his own imagined notoriety! In another sense, too, he may have been trying to excuse his own moral lapses by falsely blaming H. F. Lyte's mother and others. Many historical details,such as the dates of his Army appointments and adventures, are corroborated by other evidence, but there is much that cannot be proved or disproved.

The Captain portrays himself as a colourful and talented society man, an able soldier perhaps, but irresponsible and in his younger days continuously in trouble with his women and his debts. Garland's statement, page 15, that the Captain spent most of his time fishing is less than fair. The claim that at Ringwood he had 'received great civilities from the genteel inhabitants and have been invited to all their parties' is characteristic of the man. Yet one can see in Thomas Lyte, if only in the striking prose in which his life story is written, the germ of the brilliance of his celebrated son.

Captain Lyte claims that his family lost most of their wealth through their loyalty to Charles I, for which many of their possessions were

[1] *ibid.,* pp. 57–8.

confiscated. His father was bred to no profession and left to amuse himself as a country gentleman, his extravagance leading to the final collapse of the estate. Captain Lyte was the youngest of 'a great many children', of whom five survived. His father died when he was ten and he was brought up by his aunt and her husband, Mr and Mrs Gibbons of Somerton. After the aunt died Thomas Lyte's great-aunt, Mrs Worral, became his guardian. She was the half-sister of Thomas' father's mother Elizabeth Lyte (née Mohun) and was the last of the Mohuns of Fleet, Dorset.

After running away from a boarding-school at Dorchester Thomas Lyte learned navigation at a school in Weymouth and later a commission was purchased for him in the Royal Marines. He began at Chatham in November 1780 but in 1786 Mrs Worral, fearing he might be sent abroad, persuaded him to seek permission to retire on half-pay, which was granted: 'I never had any attachment to the sea'. In 1788 Mrs Worral died and Thomas missed her 'as if she had really been my mother'. She left him £1,200 (most of her estate) and her executor Mr Templeman of Dorchester suggested he might enter the Church; his name was entered at a college. Thomas found the preparatory study under a tutor too hard, however, and without consulting Templeman he purchased an Army commission, withdrew his name from the college, dismissed his tutor and returned to Dorchester!

He then fell in love with Templeman's daughter Charlotte, whose wealth would help him get on in the Army, and planned to marry her when he had been promoted Captain. Finding he had no hope of promotion, however, he sold his commission, after which Templeman prevented Charlotte from having any more to do with him. Thomas Lyte therefore planned to spend a summer in Scotland to recover his health and dispel grief. At this time (1790) he chanced to meet at a party in London a very pretty girl aged about twenty, Anna Maria Oliver, who had previously been introduced to him at Chatham as a young widow of modest means. He persuaded her to accompany him and a servant on a ship to Scotland. He claims to have found out later that she had not been previously married but had been living with a man. They took a house 'near the best shooting-ground in East Lothian' and the next spring they moved to Berwick-on-Tweed, where their first child Thomas Mohun was born on 6 January 1792.

Thomas Lyte claimed that he and Anna Maria were never married. They were certainly accepted for some years as man and wife in the elegant circles in which they loved to mix, and for this reason it has been argued that they were legally married according to Scottish law.[1] No one has asserted that the couple went through a marriage ceremony. In fairness to Anna Maria, it seems unlikely that Thomas Lyte should have believed her to be a widow when she can only have been eighteen or nineteen on first meeting him at Chatham. Henry Francis Lyte had the greatest respect for his mother, and both his daughter and a granddaughter were called Anna Maria.

In May 1792 Thomas Lyte and Anna Maria moved to Tillmouth, ten miles from Berwick. 'Here I resolved to live very economically as the ready money left me by my Aunt was nearly expended . . . I sold my Horse and Gig and contented myself with a Poney', the Captain records. After a year there Sir Francis Blake, Lord of the Manor, required the house, so the Lytes moved to The Cottage, Ednam, near Kelso in Roxburghshire.

Ednam is a charming village in beautiful countryside. The Lytes' house, now called Ednam West Mains, still stands there largely unchanged in its exterior, beside the River Eden bridge. Here Henry Francis Lyte was born on 1 June 1793. The village was already noted as the birthplace of the poet James Thomson, author of 'Rule, Britannia', whose father was the parish minister. On 13 June the infant H. F. Lyte was baptised at the parish church.

[1] see p. 33 below.

2

EARLY DAYS

BORN as it seemed in idyllic surroundings, the young Henry Francis Lyte was soon to know the sadness which embraced so much of his life and which is often reflected in the words of his poems and hymns. On his own admission Thomas Lyte heartily regretted his elopement with Anna Maria, even at the time Henry Francis was born. A sense of the responsibilities of parenthood kept the family together for a few more years, however, and in March 1795 a third son, George John, was born to the couple at Ednam. The previous May Thomas Lyte, finding it necessary to increase his income, had returned to the Army as a lieutenant in the Southern Fencibles, a Scottish regiment commanded by the Earl of Hopetoun. Lyte claimed that he had been awarded the Freedom of Edinburgh when with this regiment in 1795 he and his men had bravely removed twenty barrels of gunpowder (which Lyte had told the soldiers were casks of whisky!) stored at the Goldsmiths' Hall where there was a very serious fire.[1] There is certainly no evidence that he lacked courage or competence as a soldier.

In the spring of 1796, feeling that his promotion was too slow, he resigned this commission and soon after became a lieutenant in the Roxburgh Fencible Cavalry. After brief postings to Newmarket and to Manchester the regiment was ordered to Ireland, where the Rebellion had just broken out, and they embarked at Liverpool in June 1797. The following December he was at long last promoted Captain. He held various postings in Ireland and seems to have fought quite well against the French, who had landed to help the Irish in August 1798. The British were slow to attack the French, Captain Lyte wrote, but finally the latter were defeated and surrendered.

Increasingly Thomas Lyte longed to rid himself of Anna Maria, who seems to have caused him embarrassment by following him almost

[1] The Freedom of the City was not officially conferred before 1813, the City Archivist reports (letter, 11.5.1972) but some of the details of the incident, including the presence of the Southern Fencibles, are confirmed in local documents.

everywhere he was posted. Once when he was moved to Ballyshannon
Maria secretly went on ahead of him and established herself at the new
depot even before he had arrived! Captain Lyte accuses her of alcoholism
and unbecoming behaviour in public, but there is no confirmation of
this in other sources and he may well have imputed bad conduct to her so
as to justify his own waywardness.

Soon the couple separated permanently. The separation clearly took
place between 1799 and 1802, and Walter Maxwell-Lyte's suggestion
of 1800 or 1801 best fits the evidence. At the time they were living at
Dunmore, Galway, where Captain Lyte was still on Army service, now
with the Northumberland Fencibles. In 1800 Maria Lyte had disposed
of the house at Ednam at Captain Lyte's request and had brought the
three sons to Ireland. When Maria realised that Lyte was determined to
part from her she agreed to go to London, taking the youngest son
George with her, hoping to find suitable work. Captain Lyte claims that
he made her an allowance of £40 p.a. but soon stopped this on hearing
that she had not got a respectable position. The latter statement is open to
doubt, however, as a letter from Maria sent by a Mrs Williams of Ballyshannon to the Headmaster of Portora while H. F. Lyte was at this school
stated that Maria had been working as a nurse in a London Hospital
several years before.

Little is known of Anna Maria's subsequent years. She was alive as late
as 1830, when she wrote a woeful letter to Captain Lyte asking him to
tell her where her children were.[1] Garland, page 15, states that eventually
she went to live with a friend, Maggie Braithwaite, at Saltburn, Yorkshire where she died. A search of the Burial Registers of Brotton and
Marske-by-Sea (which parishes then covered the Saltburn area) has
failed to produce evidence of her death. H. F. Lyte as far as we know
never saw his mother again. He enquired several times as to her whereabouts but with no success. Garland, page 18, states that H. F. Lyte,
unable to understand why his mother never wrote to him 'could only
surmise that she had gone to a happier place, which was the case', but this
cannot be right as it refers to a period long before 1830.

Thomas Lyte soon found another spouse. In June 1802, the Irish
Rebellion being over, his regiment was due to be disbanded and he was

[1] Sir Henry Maxwell-Lyte had a theory that the date of this letter, though clearly
    written, was a mistake, and that Maria died years before 1830. Like Walter
    Maxwell-Lyte we do not think this feasible, though we had the Burial Registers
    searched back to 1810.

All Saints' Church, Brixham, built on the site of Lower Brixham Church and completed in 1907

Berry Head House, 1973   By courtesy of the Berry Head House Hotel

detached to Roscommon. There on 1 October 1802 he married Eliza Naghten, an orphan girl who he thought would be content 'with the few enjoyments my humble income would afford', and who, for the first few years at any rate 'was everything I could wish her'. The Roscommon Church Registers prior to 1845 were destroyed in the 1922 uprising when the Four Courts in Dublin, where they were stored, were blown up. So the marriage entry cannot be checked, but there is little doubt that the couple were married at Roscommon that day. Captain Lyte states so categorically, and thereafter always refers to Eliza as 'my wife', a term he never uses for Maria. Furthermore he remained with Eliza until her death in 1829 (though he confesses to being the father of another woman's child once after the marriage) and she bore him eight children. If, as he claims, he never went through a marriage ceremony with Maria Oliver there would have been no difficulty over the 'second' marriage, but even if he had been legally married to her he was far enough away to be able to commit bigamy without fear of detection.

Captain Lyte had kept his house at Ballyshannon, where it appears that the two sons lived for the first year or two after their mother's departure. In October 1803 the two boys were sent by their father to Portora Royal School, Enniskillen, as boarders. The Headmaster, Dr Robert Burrowes (later Dean of Cork), wrote the same month to the new Mrs Lyte: 'I have had the honor of a letter from Captain Lyte desiring to know whether I have at present room to accommodate two young gentlemen his sons and pointing out the mode of education they should receive.'[1] The Headmaster hoped that the boys could begin that term.

Portora was one of the well-known public schools founded in Ulster early in the seventeenth century.[2] Originally at nearby Ballybalfour, the school moved to Enniskillen in 1641. In 1777 new premises were built by Noble on Portora Hill to house seventy boarders, these buildings forming the central block of the old school campus. In those days the government of the school was in the hands of the King and Viceroy; since 1890 it has had a board of governors. It is beautifully situated on the shores of Lough Erne which with its bathing, boating and innumerable islands alive with wildfowl was always a delight. In the centre of the lough stands Devenish Island with its ruined chapel. The school numbers amongst its old boys Archbishop William Magee of Dublin and Lords Chancellors Plunket and Whiteside.

[1] Lyte family papers.
[2] Details from *The Public and Preparatory Schools Yearbook, 1972* and a letter from the Rev. D. L. Graham to W. Maxwell-Lyte, 18.8.1947 (Portora papers).

In Lyte's time there were only twelve boarders who had to rise at 5.30 a.m. and begin their studies at 6 a.m.[1] Dr Burrowes was a most successful Head and the school pulled up rapidly under his leadership.

Previously a Fellow of Trinity College, Dublin, he was a firm but kindly man, a competent scholar who tried hard to impart to his pupils his lofty ideals of life and conduct. A fellow-student of Lyte's, both at Portora and at Trinity College, Dublin, describes the Lyte brothers' arrival at the school thus:[2]

'In the year 1804 (sic) a postchaise arrived and deposited two boys dressed in very old tartan jackets who were reported to the school to be the sons of an officer quartered in the town of Sligo, and more than this was never ascertained about their parentage by their school-fellows, and of the parent who had sent them, on the eve of departure for foreign service, to the care of Dr Burrowes. Nothing further was heard until (between two and three years after) his station abroad was ascertained.

Thomas, the elder of the boys, came to be traditionally regarded in the school as being almost a simpleton but Henry soon proved himself endowed with abilities, really amounting to genius, so brilliant and various that he eclipsed all competitors. An opportunity presenting itself Dr Burrowes transmitted the helpless elder brother to his father, but the younger he retained under his kind-hearted guardianship until his pupil had attained to a position in the University which led to independence.

Henry Lyte's enviable pre-eminence and ascendancy above his companions must have been associated with great amiability; for though somewhat singular in habit, he was popular with his school-fellows and left behind him the reputation of a boy of extraordinary talent, desultory and flighty, eccentric but very amiable. He entered College in 1809, obtaining one of the sizarships of the year, and afterwards a scholarship both on distinguished answering.'

Captain Lyte's autobiography confirms that at this time he was ordered to Jersey. His previous regiment, the Northumberland Fencibles, had been disbanded in 1802, leaving him without a job. In his own words: 'My brother and friends endeavoured to get me an Army post . . . and I one evening perceived my name, very unexpectedly, in the Gazette as

[1] W. Copeland Trimble, speech at the Unveiling of Lyte's Portrait at the School (Portora papers).

[2] G. A. Grierson, *Notes and Queries,* 2nd Series, 1859, Vol. 7, p. 182.

Captain in the 1st Battalion of the Army of Reserve. Thus I was by the goodness of Providence rescued from poverty and distress.' He added that he still owed £60–£70 in Ireland and had not enough money even to fit himself out as an officer. Needless to say he never paid any fees for his sons at Portora. He claims that his youngest son George was in a destitute state in London, having been deserted by his mother, so that he was obliged to pay for the boy's board and clothing. Later he sent George to a Yorkshire academy. Mrs Williams of Ballyshannon in her letter to Dr Burrowes, however, quotes Maria Lyte as having written that George had been taken from her.

War Office records show[1] that Lyte's new regiment, soon to be renamed the 1st Garrison Battalion, was moved to Jersey in December 1803, five months after he had joined it. He and his new wife stayed at London and at Gravesend for a short spell before travelling to Jersey. They lived there until 1818, Captain Lyte undertaking various military and civilian jobs during his fourteen years on the Island. While there he wrote *A Sketch of the History and Present State of the Island of Jersey,* published in 1808. It is a slim volume of 109 pages, of no great substance and rather in the style of a guide-book, though without illustrations.

In 1818 the Lytes retired to Ringwood, Hampshire, Captain Lyte having to leave Jersey secretly, for fear of his creditors. He admits that had he stayed any longer he might have been gaoled for debt under Jersey laws; none the less his Obituary notice in the *Jersey Times and Military Chronicle* (2 August 1850) says: 'The deceased was for many years a respected resident of this Island, and was the father of Mr T. O. Lyte of 14 Colomberie-street, St Helier.' A descendant of Mr T. O. Lyte, Mr B. E. N. Lyte, still owns a house in Jersey, though for some years there has been no Lyte permanently resident there. In November 1828 Captain Lyte and his family moved again to Purewell, Christchurch, Hampshire, where Eliza Lyte died in 1829. Captain Lyte himself died there on 26 July 1850 and was buried at Christchurch Priory four days later, his age being given as eighty-six in the Register.

Before returning to Henry Francis Lyte, we make brief mention of the later fortunes of his brothers. Captain Lyte records that he sent the elder brother Thomas to the East Indies, 'where for some years he got on well but taking to liquor lost all that he had gained'. A letter from F. Bishop of Madras to H. F. Lyte, 3 September 1819, states that Lyte's brother

[1] Letter from Ministry of Defence (Central and Army) Librarian to the author, July 1971.

(presumably Thomas) had recently been promoted Conductor of Ordnance in the Cattle Department under the Commissariat, the appointment being 'one of respectability with an income suitable thereto'. Bishop had received the most favourable assurances of the brother's 'invariable Correct Conduct'. Thomas died at Brixham in 1831 aged thirty-nine. According to Sir Henry Maxwell-Lyte's notes, Thomas, who never married, returned from India in 1831 and went to see his father in Hampshire, dying 'a few days later' at Berry Head.[1]

George, the youngest brother, wrote to H. F. Lyte from Hamburg in June 1820: 'I am now on board of a vessell that is going to Bahia in the Braziels (now in Ecuador) from whence if it lays in my Power I shall make the Best of my way to America.' John Maxwell-Lyte's letter to his brother Walter, ca. 1947, states that George died in 1820.

We now resume the story of H. F. Lyte, who had been left by his father at Portora Royal School. Garland's statement, page 15, that at seven years old Henry was alone in the world and not able to contact his parents is incorrect. He was in fact ten when his father left for Jersey and later he met Captain Lyte again on a number of occasions, some of which will be mentioned. For years H. F. Lyte was given to understand that Captain Lyte was his uncle. Walter Maxwell-Lyte supposed that in order to cover up his first marriage, if marriage it was, Captain Lyte described his second wife to the children as their aunt, and later gently transposed his own status from that of father to that of uncle. The denouement between father and son did not take place, according to Sir Henry Maxwell-Lyte, until 29 April 1818. This was just after H. F. Lyte had been making enquiries about his baptism and parentage. It seems strange that Dr Burrowes, who practically adopted the boy, did not tell him about his parentage but he may have concealed the facts from kindly motives.

It would be hard to describe Henry Francis Lyte's feelings during those early years at Portora. As Garland points out, Lyte's poem 'On Dreaming of My Mother',[2] with its touching lines beginning 'Stay, gentle shadow of my mother, stay', clearly shows the great affection he cherished for his mother. He must have missed her greatly, and his father was nearly always away. Yet he settled down well at Portora, where as far as we know he spent his school holidays as well as the terms. Dr Burrowes was

[1] So it is stated in Sir Henry Maxwell-Lyte's notes, but at the time the Lytes were living at Burton House, not Berry Head.
[2] H. F. Lyte, Poems, Chiefly Religious, 2nd edition, 1841, p. 160; see p. 157 below.

obviously a splendid guardian and quite apart from financing Henry Francis he did everything he could to foster his talents. In a letter he wrote to Lyte years later in 1818, Burrowes declared: 'I am highly gratified by your success in life and by finding your principles those which I deeply lament I often fail in inculcating.'[1] This letter was in reply to one from Lyte asking to repay his school and college fees which Burrowes had so generously provided. Burrowes accepted the offer but typically added 'on no account deprive yourself or Mrs Lyte of the smallest gratification'.

Garland, page 15, states that before Dr Burrowes took over the financial responsibility for the two Lyte brothers a Miss Mc.Innes befriended them and did her best to look after them, but being in straitened circumstances herself was about to put them in a Poor Law Institution when Dr Burrowes decided to become their guardian. We have not found any other authority for this statement.

It was not only the care of his guardian and the congenial company of his schoolfellows that made life tolerable for the young Henry Francis Lyte. He delighted in the glorious natural surroundings in which Portora was placed. From his earliest youth he had an intense love of nature. Not only is this mirrored in the large number of poems he wrote on the beauties of the countryside; equally it is shown in the vivid prose descriptions of Swiss alpine scenery in his diaries. 'It is impossible to describe the beauty of the spot where the magnificent Jungfrau first fronts you in its snowy grandeur' he wrote in his diary on 22 June 1827. 'Imagine on one side a cliff of immeasurable height of mingled rocks and trees, on the other a more gradual ascent of the greenest slopes covered with chalets or little cots and crowned also with timber. In the bottom of the valley behold a river foaming through the rocks, sometimes in sight, sometimes lost among the wood, the Staubbach flings down its foam over the cliffs 700 feet, and above all soars the Jungfrau with its sister alps in everlasting snow like winter in the arms of spring.' Such words, written in great haste in odd moments during a tiring 800 mile return journey from Dieppe to Geneva, testify more than any facts could do to the poet's immense love of the beauties of land and sea and sky.

Even at school Lyte's poetic gift was beginning to flourish. His first manuscript book of poems bears the date 1805 on the title page, Henry Francis then being twelve.[2] His well-known poem 'Ode to a Primrose' is

[1] Lyte family papers.
[2] Walter Maxwell-Lyte, letters to Rev. D. L. Graham (Headmaster of Portora) 13.10.1947 and 16.10.1947 (Portora papers).

apparently dated 1808 in the manuscript book and 1812 in the published poem. Walter Maxwell-Lyte believed that it was at any rate partly written at Portora. Even before this he wrote 'The Robin Redbreast', which he evidently thought was of insufficient merit to publish with his first book of poems in 1833. It bears the heading 'On hearing one sing near my window one rainy day in autumn' and the footnote 'One of the first regular copies of verse I ever wrote—H. F. Lyte'. In all probability it was written at Portora soon after Lyte was twelve. There are six verses, one being:

> True I may pine and shrink awhile
>   Upon the leafless spray
> But soon enlivening spring shall smile
>   And all again be gay
> The woods shall bloom, the fields be fair
>   And blue the sunny sky
> And all in water, earth and air
>   Rejoice as well as I.

In springtime the surrounds of Lough Erne are a veritable carpet of primroses and buttercups, bluebells and daisies, amidst lovely woods and mountains, and grass as green as only Ireland knows. A newspaper article written in 1926 describes the beautiful scenery the boy would have seen on the long and interesting journey from Ednam to Portora.[1] In fact the Lytes had left Ednam long before Henry started at Portora, but even so this graphic account gives some idea of the delights he would have experienced in those sad yet treasured years at Enniskillen. The same article describes Lyte as a studious youth of pale oval face and luminous eyes who loved to loiter in the woods or thoughtfully wander with kindred companions along the shores of Lough Erne. Walter Maxwell-Lyte pictures him as walking alone through woods in lovely countryside, pencil and notebook in his hand.[2]

Little more is known of Lyte's Portora days but he was clearly very successful at his studies and when only sixteen he gained a Sizarship at his Headmaster's old college, beginning at Dublin University in May 1809. As Sizar he had to perform certain menial duties such as waiting on the Fellows' table and sweeping floors,[3] which he undertook cheerfully. He rapidly grew in stature both as a scholar and as a person. By now he was six feet two inches high, remarkably handsome with dark auburn curly

[1] F. J. Bigger, *Belfast Evening Telegraph*, 22.3.1926.
[2] W. Maxwell-Lyte, *British Weekly*, 3.4.1947.
[3] Letter to the author from Trinity College, Dublin, Information Office, 17.11.1971.

hair, withal modest but a brilliant and witty speaker and a poet of considerable ability.[1]

Lyte added to his limited income by taking private pupils,[2] and in 1813 he won a university scholarship, being placed first on the list of twenty-four successful candidates.[3] Three years running he won the Chancellor's Prize for English Verse with his poems 'The Battle of Salamanca', 'The Peace' and 'Richard Coeur de Lion'. In the latter case he was commanded to recite 200 lines of the poem before the Chancellor, who liked it so well that he asked for the whole work for perusal—'This I, with my usual dilatoriness, have not yet sent him'.[4] The Provost expressed a wish that he should publish the poem, dedicated to the Vice-Chancellor and 'at the desire of the Board and Fellows of the University'. In February 1814, when still under twenty-one, he graduated Bachelor of Arts.

While at Trinity College his cultural interests and friendly manner led to many lasting friendships, especially that with John Kerr, a poet like himself. These two corresponded throughout most of Lyte's life, many of their letters to each other being in the form of poems. One such letter, dated 1812 and 'addressed to my friend J.K.' is quoted in the *Remains*, page ix. It describes Lyte's nostalgia for the evenings he used to enjoy with his poetical circle in Dublin.

> And then those nights, those Attic nights we've pass'd,
> With the fond few who felt and thought as we,
> Chiding the hours that stole away so fast,
> On wings of reason, wit, and minstrelsy:
> When my young muse would list and learn from thee
> Strains she had envied any tongue but thine,
> Or from discussions fanciful and free,
> On books, men, things gay, moral, and divine,
> Glean'd much to please and mend, enlighten and refine.

Another letter, written by Lyte to Kerr in 1840, appears in his published poems under the title 'Stanzas to J.K.'[5]

On gaining his degree Lyte's first inclination was to train as a physician and he studied medicine for some months in 1814. Soon, however, he felt a stronger calling to the ministry of the Church of England and Ireland, and abandoned his medical studies altogether.

[1] W. Maxwell-Lyte, British Weekly, 3.4.1947.
[2] *Remains,* p. ix.
[3] See footnote 3, p. 12.
[4] H. F. Lyte, letter to J. Kerr, March 1815, quoted in *Remains,* p. xiv.
[5] *Remains,* p. 5.

LYTE'S FIRST YEARS IN THE MINISTRY

ON 10 DECEMBER 1814 the Rt Rev. Percy Jocelyn, Bishop of Leighlin and Ferns, sent Letters Dimissory[1] to the Bishop of Kilmore requesting him to ordain Lyte to the diaconate for service in Leighlin and Ferns Diocese. Lyte was duly ordained by the Bishop of Kilmore, the Rt Rev. George de la Poer Beresford, at the Advent Ordination on Sunday, 18 December 1814.[2] We may fairly assume that Lyte was delighted to be made deacon (probably in Kilmore Cathedral) in the diocese where his beloved Enniskillen was situate, close to his 'home' and friends. On Michaelmas Day (a Friday) 1815 he was ordained Priest by Bishop Jocelyn in Ferns Cathedral.[1] Lyte was only twenty-one when he was made deacon, which was unusual and normally required a special Faculty.[3]

Lyte's training for the ministry was very short, for he was made deacon only ten months after his graduation and part of this brief period was spent reading medicine. Such training as he had would certainly have been at Trinity College, Dublin. The Church of England and Ireland at this time required little formal training if the ordinand was a graduate of good standing in his home district. The Irish Bishops had in fact in 1790 bound themselves not to ordain in future any man 'who did not produce certificates of attendance upon the lectures given by the Professor of Divinity, the Divinity Lecturer, and the Assistant Lecturer in Divinity'. The Bishops had at the same time forwarded to the Board of Trinity College a list of books, knowledge of which would be required of all their ordinands.[4] No doubt Lyte was able to fulfil the requirements, which were not great, during his time at Trinity College.

For his first curacy Lyte was licensed to the parish of Taghmon, a small country village seven miles from Wexford in the south-east corner of

[1] The Letters Dimissory, Lyte's Letter of Priest's Orders and his Licence to the Curacy of Taghmon (dated 20.2.1815) are all amongst the family papers.
[2] Ordinations in Kilmore Diocese, Reynell MSS., Vol. I, Belfast Diocesan Library.
[3] Letter from Rev. G. Browne to W. Maxwell-Lyte, 17.6.1947, quoting Archdeacon J. R. Willis.
[4] Oulton, *The Study of Divinity in Trinity College, Dublin,* 1941, p. 15.

Ireland. Here Lyte assisted the Rector, Prebendary Simon Little, although strangely enough neither ever signed the Parish Registers, which were usually signed by another curate, George Richards. There was the single church of St Munnu, which was small and was rebuilt by the Board of First Fruits in 1818, just after Lyte had left.[1] There is a memorial plaque to Lyte in the church. Lyte was only in the parish about eighteen months, yet this brief spell was to be of considerable significance for his future ministry. He described his experiences in 'this dreary curacy' (as he elsewhere styled it) in a letter to John Kerr dated March 1815:[2]

'Here I had at first settled "remote from towns" in almost perfect seclusion, giving myself up to the duties of my situation, writing my sermons, visiting my sick, catechizing my children, without other companions than my flute, my pen and my books. This answered very well for a little time, while I had plenty of occupation on my hands.

However, it was too great a change from the comfort, the society and the carelessness which I had before enjoyed, to be long capable of satisfying my wishes. I found myself obliged to submit to constant intrusions, to attend long, formal dinner-parties, to take long rides at night, or give up the best part of my time to my neighbours, and other miseries which I had not taken into account, when I had resolved upon living "passing rich", &c., in seclusion. All this, with some other causes also, determined me to attend to the solicitations of my old friend B. (*sc.* Mr Thomas Bell) to continue in my care of his boys, and in my partaking his home and society. I am now settled again with him.'

While living with the Bells, Lyte continued to minister at Taghmon Church on Sundays; according to Garland, page 20, he took the Service of Thanksgiving there for the victory at Waterloo.

It may be thought that the young Lyte was somewhat self-centred and intolerant, even by the standards of modern curates, to write in this vein after no more than three months in his first curacy! We must allow for the fact that he was still only twenty-one, however, and he had first felt a firm vocation to the ministry not even a year previously. Furthermore a deep change in his attitude was on the horizon, as we shall soon learn. The most interesting feature of this letter is perhaps Lyte's natural taste for elegant company and gracious living at such an early age, and this despite the

[1] S. Lewis, *Topographical Dictionary of Ireland,* 1837, p. 586.
[2] *Remains,* p. xiv.

stern privations of his childhood years. Here he shows a definite affinity with his ancestors and particularly with his father. Like Captain Lyte, Henry Francis always seemed to be able to enjoy the comforts of the rich. Even in those moments when poverty seemed to be staring him in the face his father's 'Providence' always seemed to rescue him at the very last minute! It is only fair to add that his flair for the company of the upper classes was in later years tempered by a very real care for the downcast and the poor.

In another letter, written to Kerr on 30 March 1818 from Marazion,[1] Lyte describes his life with the Bells: 'Here I lived for some time, comfortably enough, assisting him in taking care of his two sons, riding about, shooting, dancing, and attending my curacy every Sunday.' Clearly the Bells' house was fairly close to Taghmon, and we may surmise that Lyte had previously acted as tutor to the boys during his time at Trinity College, perhaps living with the family during vacations. Lyte apparently served as *full-time* curate of Taghmon for no more than two months, since he had already taken up residence with the Bells by March 1815. Garland, page 20, describes this latter phase as follows: 'We see him for a short period entering into various worldly pursuits which for a time lessened his religious interest and his search for higher things.'

Obviously Lyte's sense of vocation was vague at this early stage. Perhaps he felt an indefinable desire to do something good in life, coupled with a belief in God as revealed by Christ which was much more part of the social background in 1815 than it is to-day. But now was to come the most far-reaching change in Lyte's outlook in the whole of his life. He describes it in the same letter to Kerr. The original seems to have been lost, but the fullest extract is given in an article by Walter Maxwell-Lyte.[2]

'From this motley round of occupations I was however withdrawn by a circumstance which led the way to all my future wanderings. A neighbouring clergyman, with whom I was intimate, and who bore the highest character for benevolence, piety and good sense, was taken ill and sent for me—I went to attend him, and witnessed all the workings of his mind and body for some weeks till he expired. I shall never forget some of the circumstances that took place, his serious and anxious inquiries into the evidence on which a future state existed, his examination into the grounds on which the Scripture stood as an authentic revelation, and his conviction that it was a just

---

[1] *Remains*, p. xvi.
[2] *The Life of Faith*, 12.11.1947.

statement of that which is and is to be. All seemed to pass before him as he stood just on the confines of eternity, as strong and distinct realities, as the parts of a picture rather than of an abstract speculation. These preliminaries settled, his inquiry next was the means by which a happy eternity was to be attained; and here indeed my blood almost curdled to hear the dying man declare and prove with the most irrefutable clearness, that both he and I had been utterly mistaken in the means we had adopted for ourselves, and recommended to others, if the explanatory Epistles of St Paul were to be taken in their plain and literal sense. You can hardly perhaps conceive the effect of all this proceeding from such a man in such a situation. I almost can fancy that I hear him now, in his own firm, earnest tone of voice saying, "But, Sir, I feel that the soul is distinct from the body, and that it may live, when its shell is rotting. Look at this hand, it is dead, and this body is all weakness, and yet my mind is as strong as it was at its best day. Sir, I am satisfied that my spirit shall survive my substance. And when I look into that volume and consider its simple majesty, its consistency, its depth, its style, its moral character, and that of its authors, I am convinced, Sir, that it is the book of God. The infinite probabilities by which it is supported convince me; and when I meet with such declarations as I do in its pages, it is not for a dying man like me, for one who is just about to make the fearful experiment of its truth, to be otherwise than in earnest about such matters". The poor man died, I rejoice to say, happy under the belief, that though he had deeply erred, there was One whose death and sufferings would atone for his delinquencies, and be accepted for all that he had incurred. I was greatly affected by the whole matter, and brought to look at life and its issue with a different eye than before, and I began to study my Bible and preach in another manner than I had previously done. There were four or five clergymen in my neighbourhood whom I had before laughed at, along with others, as Methodists, and whom I deemed enthusiastic rhapsodists, weak simpletons, unable rationally to defend their tenets, because they did not choose to take the trouble of doing so, but rather to toil away, and take patiently whatever reproaches fell upon them. These men I now saw to be (generally speaking) in the right; and I did my utmost to follow their example.'

Garland's comment on this situation, page 22, is: 'Lyte was at this phase of his life between two fires; one the orthodox and dogmatic teachings of the clerical scholars of the day, and the other the more simple and practical philosophy as expounded by Christ.' This, however, is to miss the point. Lyte was an able scholar and always interested in academic theology; much of his library was devoted to this subject. Even so, he was far too much a Romantic to be captivated by sheer dogma. His change of heart is a clear case of what we should call to-day an Evangelical 'conversion'. Wesley had died only twenty-five years before, the Catholic revival had yet to become articulate, and the air was full of the fruits of Evangelical Anglican and Methodist revivalists. We may suppose that Lyte, like thousands before and after him, came to see the Epistle to the Romans in a new light. Previously, perhaps, he had thought of the Christian life largely in terms of good works carried out by divine grace in response to our Lord's example; now he saw the vital importance of faith (in the sense of a childlike trust in God and in the redeeming power of Christ's sacrifice) which would first give him the feeling of acquittal from past sin, after which the Holy Spirit would help him forward to even greater heights of sanctification. Lyte set out this viewpoint fairly clearly in his Saltram sermon in 1823.

Who was the dying priest? None of the surviving documents names him and it seems impossible, short of new evidence being uncovered, to establish his identity with certainty. In 1947 Canon G. Browne, then Rector of Horetown with Taghmon, did a considerable amount of research on the matter for Walter Maxwell-Lyte and we can hardly improve on this. Only two priests died within twenty-five miles of Taghmon in or about 1816; they were the Rev. Abraham Swanne, Rector of Killurin (six miles from Taghmon) and the Rev. John Jacob, Curate of Ardcolm (twelve miles from Taghmon). Both died in 1816 leaving a widow and children. The local tradition in Taghmon, as the present Rector the Rev. Ernest Brandon bears out, is that Jacob was the dying priest. This story may well have arisen, however, because Jacob's son Preb. T. J. J. Jacob was buried at Taghmon and his family gave a lectern to the church. There is no evidence to connect Lyte with Jacob, except that Lyte's friends the Le Huntes lived in Ardcolm parish. Although Canon Browne is understandably reluctant to disown the local tradition, he himself cites far more evidence in favour of Swanne. After Swanne died on 8 February 1816, Lyte took the chair at the Easter Vestry at Killurin on 16 April 1816, and at another Vestry a fortnight later, the minutes being in his handwriting. Lyte also took baptisms at Killurin on 25 February and 7 March that year, and a wedding on 18 April, and actually signed the Registers in all three cases 'Henry F. Lyte, Curate'. Swanne died at fifty-four, leaving at least three children, two of whom (Annabella and Gilbert) both died in 1878, so that they must have been tiny when their father died. Thus it seems highly probable that Swanne was the dying priest.

Though Garland does not name this priest, later in his book, page 50, he gives a peculiar doublet of the story involving a priest called John Patterson: 'A great turning point with regard to Lyte's views on immortality came when he underwent a remarkable psychic experience. One of his dearest friends, a brother clergyman from a neighbouring parish, called John Patterson died, and upon his death this friend appeared in a vision to Lyte and told him that he had passed into another state of life and would not be able to visit him again in the body as was usual. The great experience of seeing and being able to speak to this friend completely altered Lyte's ideas on death.' Garland quotes what seems to be a letter of Lyte's (undated and apparently now lost) on the vision:

> 'I wrote those early hymns not from inner knowledge but from the knowledge of theological learning, and if you will care to look at and examine these poems you will see how different they are to those written later. When I wrote "Jesus, I my cross have taken", I thought that the ill-health I had was my cross and I did not realise at the time that my cross would be my own conscience. If one follows closely my poems on the Psalms one can learn many lessons therefrom. It was after I had acquired this inner knowledge that I was able to see clearly my own path and my own mistakes, and though my life became increasingly difficult on account of my ill-health which became worse, we were in the little fishing village of Brixham very happy. I had left Marazion behind, and if you will examine my poems after I had arrived at Brixham, that dear little church, you will see that I had endeavoured to put into those writings that which I not only now felt, but the sorrows for what I had not done before. I trust you will not think that I have any other motive in telling you this than to show you the awfulness of learning without knowledge.'

This correspondence rather suggests that Lyte had the vision a year or two *after* leaving Taghmon, and it does not seem as if John Patterson was the same man as the dying priest to whom Lyte ministered in Ireland. Strangely enough we have been quite unable to trace John Patterson's name in any church records. Irish Church Registers[1] give no mention of a priest of this name serving anywhere near Taghmon at the time. We have searched the records of all Institutions in Exeter Diocese from 1807–26, and all Curates' Licences issued by the Bishop of Exeter from 1811–29, without finding any trace of the elusive John Patterson. The Winchester Diocesan Archivist cannot trace him, nor does his name occur in the lists of graduates of Oxford and Cambridge Universities, so his identity must remain a mystery. Nevertheless Lyte's letter is well worth recording for the depth of spiritual understanding shown.

After the death of the priest living near Taghmon, Lyte felt duty-bound to help his widow and family. 'I had also the care of all the concerns of my friend's widow and young family', he wrote to Kerr,[2] 'which I arranged for them by incessant exertion for four months. The excessive labour of mind and body which these concomitant circumstances brought upon me, soon proved too much for my constitution, already enfeebled by my attendance on my dying friend. I felt into a rapid decline, and was ordered immediately to leave the country for the Continent, if I wished to live.' Lyte's chest illness, of which this was the first recorded sign as far as we know, was to dog him for the rest of his life and ultimately brought about his death. It was recognised throughout that he suffered from asthma; at some stage difficult to date tuberculosis set in.

In order to recuperate from this illness Lyte went on a horseback tour in France with a friend called Lewis, who was a lieutenant in the Royal Engineers. Walter Maxwell-Lyte's notes state that the tour lasted from September 1816 until the following summer. A further section of Lyte's letter to Kerr, quoted only as far as we know in Sir Henry Maxwell-Lyte's notes, adds: 'I was supplied with money (*sc.* for this holiday) by a friend, and set sail for Jersey—There I found our uncle, the only immediate relative that I have, with the exception of a brother who is abroad.' The 'uncle' was obviously his father, Captain Thomas Lyte, who remained in Jersey until 1818, and who H. F. Lyte had supposed was his uncle until Captain Lyte revealed his true relationship in the latter year. The Captain states in his autobiography that H. F. Lyte visited him in Jersey in 1816 and that he was 'a very clever young man'. H. F. Lyte actually stood as godfather to Francis Henry Lyte, a son born to the Captain and his wife Eliza, on 30 September 1816, during this visit and the contact led Lyte

[1] Letter from the Church of Ireland Representative Church Body Library, Dublin, 8.2.1972.
[2] *Remains,* p. xviii.

later to invite the Captain and his youngest daughter Harriet to stay with him and his wife at Marazion.

Part of the tour, dating from 7–22 October 1816, is covered by a diary, written in Lyte's tiny handwriting in an ordinary pocket-sized notebook. The diary commences with Lyte and Lewis setting sail from Jersey in the small open cutter of Captain Madieu of Cancale, with their two horses on board! They landed at Cancale and travelled on horseback via St Malo, Châteauneuf, Dinan, Rennes, Châteaubriant (where they stayed a week), Angers and St Aubins, where the diary ends. In his elegant prose Lyte describes vividly and in great detail the people he met, the buildings he visited and the scenery and local customs he saw on the journey. There is a certain sense of joyous youthful abandon about his writing at this stage and he does not show the developed religious discipline so clearly evident in the 1827 Diary. Nevertheless there are clear indications where his theological sympathies lay. On Sunday, '20' October (21 meant) at Châteaubriant he wrote:

'Ah, how different the appearance of France on Sunday from that of Scotland. The open shops, the busy populace, the mechanics often at work and, above all, the windmills on the neighbouring hills which I had been used to admire as standing still in silent homage to the Lord's day told me that I was not in my native land. I am and always, I fear, will be out of humour in France on Sundays. The waggoners and muleteers were all journeying with their loaded panniers and teams as usual and I hastened back to my lodgings. I shut myself up in my chamber away from this impious people. "O! that mine eyes were waters and my head a fountain of tears and that I had in the wilderness a lodging place" said the prophet Jeremiah at the sight of the sins of Israel, and I could make the same exclamation on a Sunday in France.'

The previous Sunday, 14 October, at Châteaubriant he had been to the 'grand Mass' at ten o'clock and was equally forthright in his views on Roman Catholic worship:

'The church was amazingly crowded and all the mummeries of the R.C.F. faithfully gone through. We had the Priest before the altar playing his antic tricks with all the dexterity of a mountebank. We had the choir trying to outnoise each other in canticles and responses, we had the habits of red and pink and blue and white, we had the bells large and small tolling and tinkling, we had the candles burning, the incense fuming, the host raised, the breast thumped, and the Father,

Son and H.G. most dexterously fugled through. I breathed up a prayer to Him who abideth not in any particular temple made with men's hands and afterwards employed myself partly in gazing at the fopperies before me, at which I could scarcely repress my smiles, partly in endeavouring to hear what the preacher said (Lyte's knowledge of French was only slight at the time), who gave us a sermon upon the horrors of revolution and the necessity for supporting the present Government.'

In other parts of the diary Lyte expressed amazement at the multitude of crosses and images scattered around the countryside, at which the local people stopped to do homage. For all his criticisms Lyte was always to some extent fascinated by the Roman Church, and in another extract (19 October, Châteaubriant) he shows at least a measure of approval of one custom of that Church:

'They have the custom here of ringing a bell for the soul of a departing person. While the struggles of death continue, a slow solemn bell is rung at intervals and when it is announced that the soul is departed a wild rapid peal is rung by another higher toned bell. The inn here is close to the church and at midnight I was awoke by this passing bell, the first I had heard in my life. I cannot describe the effect it had on me, sounding on my ear through the dark and silent night. The wild violent peal announced that all was over and left me to silence and to my own reflections. If I might judge from the effect which this ceremony occurring at such an hour produced on me I would say that there were some of the rites of the Romish Church which might have been tolerated by the Reformers without any injury to Christianity and this among their number.'

Lyte seemed very conscious at this time of the attractions of the opposite sex, and of his own attractiveness to women. Several passages from the diary are on this theme, of which we quote one of the most charming. It describes the sixteen-year-old daughter of the innkeeper at Cancale (8 October):

'She was dressed in a dark close gown with a large muslin ruff round the neck tied with a small plain ribbon . . . She had a most sweet interesting countenance, a well-made person and when we conversed or attempted to converse with her we were much struck with her modest self possession, her diffidence, her elegance and her ease. She tripped about us like a fairy on her deer-like limbs, she sang for us in the course of the day, in short she quite won my heart

and realised all that I had heard of the witchery of French ladies . . .
Slept well and dreamt of Mademoiselle.'

(9 October) 'We got up at half past six and breakfasted at eight.
The intermediate time was spent preparing for our journey and
flirting with Mademoiselle. Elle est une fille très jolie; there is
something of fairy elegance in all her movements all her words her
actions and her looks. At breakfast Mademoiselle sat next to me and
gave me a hundred kind looks and words. She certainly has one of
the most beautiful countenances I ever saw, and when set off by her
light and fancifully scattered ringlets, is quite irresistible . . . We
parted from Cancale with regret, leaving Mademoiselle in tears.'

Delightful as the young lady was, there is no record that Lyte ever
tried to get in touch with her again.

There is much more that could be quoted from this diary, of another
young lady who made an all-out attempt to engage Lyte's attentions as
he left a Roman Catholic church or of his interesting discussions with
French soldiers, including a Capitaine who attended Napoleon on the
Retreat from Moscow. The diary shows Lyte at twenty-three to be a
happy, attractive, talented young man, full of the joys of life despite his
questionable health, a very human person with a remarkably deep
understanding of life for his age. As he was always modest in describing
his achievements in other directions we suppose that he was being no
more than truthful in mentioning the various advances made to him by
attractive young ladies, one being ten years after his marriage. He seems
to have possessed all his father's personal charm, to which were added
great intellectual and poetic gifts and a deep sense of dedication.

The tour achieved its object of restoring Lyte's health, though he
remained delicate for the rest of his life. Another extract from Lyte's
letter to Kerr records: 'While I was on the Continent, I continued, with
the exception of a two months' residence in Paris, in constant motion,
according to the direction of my Physician; and the exercise, air, and
agreeable and diversified scenes I passed through, soon restored me to
my accustomed state of health. On my return to England, after a short
visit to Bristol, I came down to this part of the kingdom, as the most
likely to agree with my constitution, and after being jostled about from
one curacy to another, I at last settled as lecturer to this little town.'[1]
This was written from Marazion on 30 March 1818.

The jostling cannot have lasted long, for Lyte was elected to the

[1] *Remains*, p. xviii.

lectureship of Marazion on 24 June 1817 and took his first baptism at the church only five days later. Garland adds that on returning to England Lyte stayed with a Mr Barlow, a retired merchant living in Bristol who had a great interest in his poems. They became close friends. Lyte also formed a friendship with Barlow's daughter Julia, Garland continues. She was a woman of artistic temperament and corresponded with Lyte for the rest of his life. We shall hear again of Julia in connection with the date of 'Abide with Me'. Barlow had a brother who was an influential business man in Cornwall, and it was through his good offices, Garland tells us, that Lyte found his next work at Marazion. This information seems to have been obtained by Garland from family correspondence that cannot now be found, and although it is impossible to corroborate it we feel that it is probably true.

The Chapel of Marazion was at the time a chapel-of-ease in the parish of St Hilary, the Lecturer being technically Curate of the latter. The Chapel, dedicated to St Ervetus, though ancient (1397) was small and un-impressive. In 1892 when Marazion became a parish in its own right the building was pulled down and the present All Saints' Church erected on the same site. In Lyte's time there was no endowed stipend at all, and the Lecturer had to depend entirely on the meagre pew rents.[1] It could hardly be described as an adequate job for one of Lyte's ability and yet he was glad to take it. As a bachelor he would not have been unduly worried from the financial angle, and even in those days a priest who had to give up his post through illness could not expect to be fixed up immediately with a job just to his liking. As Lecturer, Lyte had virtually a sole charge and was in effect 'Vicar' of Marazion. A countryman at heart, he would have been delighted with the beautiful surroundings and of course he always loved the sea.

An unusual feature of the lectureship was that by 'immemorial' tradition the appointment was made by the Mayor and Corporation of the town, though always with the final consent of the Vicar of St Hilary. It is not known how this custom arose; there is no mention of it in the Royal Charter (1595) of Elizabeth I by which the Corporation was constituted. The Exeter Diocesan Registers show a number of cases of curates being nominated by other persons than the incumbent. The Proceedings of Marazion Corporation, 24 June 1817, record[1] that 'Letters being produced by the Mayor and Churchwardens from the Rev. John Marriott, the

[1] T. Reynolds, *The Churches and Chapels of Market Jew*, 1963.

Rev. W. F. Lyte (*sic*), the Rev. J. Neale and the Rev. Sampson Harris proposing themselves as Candidates, it was Resolved that the Rev. W. F. Lyte (in consequence of his now being resident in this Town) be elected to the Lectureship', and he was unanimously elected subject to the approbation of the Vicar of St Hilary. Lyte did not take up the house the Corporation had purchased for the Lecturer, so it was sold again. No doubt as a bachelor he decided to live in lodgings.

According to Reynolds,[1] Lyte's ministry at Marazion lasted from 24 June 1817 to 4 October 1819, the latter being the date of appointment of the next Lecturer, the Rev. J. H. Townsend, who remained in the curacy until 1845.[2] Lyte was not formally licensed to Marazion until 23 January 1818; on 20 November 1818 he was also licensed to the curacy of neighbouring Perranuthnoe at a stipend of £100 p.a.[3] The Sunday service at Marazion was only in the morning, so that Lyte was able to assist the Rector of Perranuthnoe at other times on Sundays and also during the week. Doubtless this additional curacy was arranged after his marriage to increase his meagre income. Strange to say, the Perranuthnoe Registers show no entry signed by Lyte *after* his licensing to that parish. In all he conducted thirteen Baptisms, Marriages or Burials at Perranuthnoe before the date of licensing; in 1817 he signed as 'Lecturer of Marazion' and after 20 September 1818 he signed simply as 'Curate'.[4]

Though Lyte's stay in Marazion was short it was a happy one. Walter Maxwell-Lyte records part of a letter H. F. Lyte wrote to a friend at the time:

'The inhabitants are a quiet ordinary kind of people, chiefly tradesmen, whom a little money saved in the till and a sprinkling of hairpowder over their heads and the capes of their coats, have transformed into gentlemen. We all live very comfortably together, and I believe that they are, in general, well pleased with their parson.'[5]

If the last few words suggest that Lyte may have been a trifle conceited, the testimonial he was given by the Vicar of St Hilary when he sought appointment as Vicar of Crediton shows clearly the high respect in which his ministry was held in the area.

Lyte remembered Marazion above all for his marriage and the birth of

[1] T. Reynolds, Local Historian, Penzance, letter to the author, 23.6.1971.
[2] Footnote 1, p. 25.
[3] Copies of the Licences may be seen in the Exeter Diocesan Archives.
[4] F. M. Richards, then Rector of Perranuthnoe, letter to W. Maxwell-Lyte, 18.10.1947.
[5] W. Maxwell-Lyte, *British Weekly*, 3.4.1947.

his first child. Anne Maxwell was staying at Marazion with her aunt, Mrs Philippa Massingberd, when Lyte met her. Their friendship ripened rapidly and they were married at Walcot (Church of England) Chapel, Bath, by Charles A. Moysey, Rector, on 21 January 1818. Though their ages were not entered in the Marriage Registers we know from Anne's burial entry at St Mary's, Brixham in 1856 and other evidence that she was 31 when she married, that is some seven years older than her husband. Garland's description of her, page 27, as austere in manner, but of a refined, gracious and gentle disposition is probably fair, and fits the only known photograph of her which is reproduced in his book. She certainly could not match her husband's good looks and personal charm, and she seems far removed in her nature and personality from the French girl who had so enchanted Lyte less than eighteen months beforehand.

Even so she had her sterling qualities, and Lyte seems to have been happy with her until the end of his days. His letters to her, even in his last years, are full of affection and almost always begin 'My dearest Anne'. She provided him with her family fortune, although he did not realise at the time of their courtship that she would be an heiress. She was an excellent house manager, trained young housemaids well so that they could later move to senior jobs, and she was good at handling finance. During Lyte's closing years of illness, the family had to plan their spending carefully so that he could winter abroad to improve his health, and here Mrs Lyte was generous in the self-sacrifice which she made. Her connections with the nobility and the 'good table' which she provided at Berry Head were a valuable asset to Lyte, and enabled him to enjoy the elegant circle of friends which meant so much to him. Mrs Lyte's different religious views—she was a keen Methodist, unfashionable as this was in those days for someone well-placed in society—probably caused her husband difficulties at times, but his tolerant nature minimized any troubles on this score. In all it was a happy and successful marriage.

One could almost write a treatise on Mrs Lyte's family connections. Her mother, who died when she was two, was the daughter of William Burrell Massingberd of South Ormesby, Lincolnshire. Her father, the Rev. William Maxwell, DD, came from a well-known Scottish-Irish family noted for their Church preferment in Ireland. One branch of the Maxwells had been honoured with the title of Baron Farnham and later (1763) the Earl of Farnham. The second Earl and fourth Baron, John James Maxwell (1760–1823) was a close friend of the Lytes, and their youngest son was named after him. He was the last Maxwell to bear the Earldom, but the Barony continues to this day.[1]

The Maxwells originally came from Calderwood, Scotland. The Very Rev. Robert Maxwell, second son of Sir John Maxwell, Kt. went to Ireland at James VI's command at the end of Elizabeth I's reign and was later appointed Dean of Armagh. His eldest son the Rt Rev. Robert Maxwell, DD became Bishop of Kilmore and Ardagh and there were other bishops in the family. Anne's great great grandfather William Maxwell was at the family seat at Falkland, Co. Monaghan during the civil war between James II and William of Orange; he was married to the sister of the Rev. George Walker who distinguished himself as Governor of Londonderry during the siege and was later killed in an ambush by Stuart supporters. Anne's grandfather the Ven. John Maxwell was Archdeacon of Clogher. Anne was her father's only surviving daughter; she had a mentally-retarded brother John, and the other children had died young. After the death of Anne's mother her father married Miss Jane Ellis; there was no issue from the second marriage.

Dr Maxwell, like many others of his day, lived a colourful life, much of which is recorded in a hand-written biography of him which Lyte wrote while at Dittisham in May 1822. He distinguished himself at Trinity College, Dublin, winning several premiums and a scholarship, being all his life an able Greek scholar. He lived from 1732 to 1818, gaining the BA degree in 1752, MA in 1755, BD and DD in 1777.[2] He spent some time at Nice, travelling there with his kinsman Lord Farnham, in order to recover from a chest infection which was considered alarming as his elder brother had died of consumption. For several years he was assistant priest at the Temple Church, London, when the Rev. Gregory Sharpe, DD was Master, and in 1775 his relative the Hon. Henry Maxwell, Bishop of Meath, appointed him to the Rectory of Mount Temple, Moate, Co. Westmeath.[3] Lyte states that the succeeding Bishop deprived him of this living later for non-residence.[4]

A fascinating claim made in 1947 both by the then Headmaster of Portora and the then Dean of St Patrick's Cathedral, Dublin is that in his early years Dr Maxwell amassed a considerable fortune from piracy,

[1] *Burke's Peerage, Baronetage and Knightage,* 104th edition, 1967, p. 926.
[2] Most of these details are from Lyte's biography of Maxwell; the degrees and dates are from the *Dictionary of National Biography,* Vol. XIII, p. 137.
[3] *Dictionary of National Biography,* Vol. XIII, p. 137.
[4] Or, according to the *Dictionary of National Biography,* he resigned the living voluntarily for the same reason.

sailing a privateer to maraud the French with the consent of the British Government.[1] The second of these two references, a newspaper article, carries the striking headline: 'Dr Maxwell of Falkland:—Squire, Pirate, Scholar, Parson'! In a letter[2] written by the Headmaster to the Dean *after* these articles were published, the former states that it is from Lyte's biography of Maxwell that the account of the piracy is drawn. It is strange, therefore, that there is no mention of it in Lyte's biography of Maxwell as we have seen it. It is just possible that the account of the piracy may have been invisibly removed, as the pages of the biography[3] (unnumbered) have all been cut out of their original exercise book and pasted to the page-stubs of another manuscript book. At any rate Lyte's biography of Dr Maxwell leaves a large gap in the middle of the latter's life un-explained, unless he simply lived in gentlemanly leisure at Falkland until fifty-six years of age. The Rev. D. L. Graham informed us that Walter Maxwell-Lyte himself told him that the piracy story was true, and Mr Jack Maxwell-Lyte his son assures us that it is universally accepted as correct amongst the Lyte family.

In 1789 at the age of fifty-six Dr Maxwell moved to Bath. According to Lyte he was driven from Falkland by the Irish Rebellion; the Dean of St Patrick's in his article added that shots were actually fired into his bedroom. At Bath he became a great friend of Dr Samuel Johnson, to whom he had been introduced in about 1755 by George Grierson, the Government printer at Dublin.[4] Lyte says that Maxwell was hardly out of Johnson's company when in London, and he thereby became acquainted with the principal literary characters of the Metropolis. He wrote Chapter 24 of Boswell's *Life of Johnson*. Graham in his note added that Maxwell became a more sincere imitator of Johnson than Boswell himself: 'He copied all his bad habits, rolling gait, unpleasant table manners, manner of dress and so on, and lived on at Bath as the doctor's ghost until the 19th century.'

Lyte only met Maxwell shortly before the latter's death, when he went to ask the hand of his daughter. Maxwell's reply was: 'Well, Sir, there is the child, and as you like one another and I see no objection to the match

---

[1] Rev. D. L. Graham, *Irish Times,* 21.11.1947 and Very Rev. D. Wilson, *Church of Ireland Gazette,* 5.12.1947.

[2] Letter of 12.12.1947, Portora papers.

[3] Its full title is: 'Sketch of the Life, as far as I am acquainted with it, of my Father-in-law Dr Maxwell and of some others of the Maxwell Family'. Written at Dittisham, May 1822.

[4] *Dictionary of National Biography,* loc. cit.

do as you chuse, only with regard to the settlement you must let me do what I chuse also.' At this time Dr Maxwell was no longer able to rise from his chair without help, and he could not read; he hired a person to read for him. His memory was impaired and he was failing fast. He had even then, however, 'a blunt hearty good humour rare in someone so old', and could still quote forty or fifty lines, readily and correctly, either from Homer or various Greek prose writers. Lyte was 'highly gratified by his anecodotes and literary conversation'. Maxwell, in spite of a certain 'nearness' in financial matters, kept a large establishment of servants and a plentiful table at Bath, and was in many cases a munificent patron and friend. Lyte tells how he liked his glass, or rather his bottle, and seldom retired to bed without two bottles of port in his stomach. It was said that when one of his doctors limited him to two glasses of wine after dinner he had a large glass bought, which would hold a bottle of wine at a time! His manner was more dictatorial than many liked, 'yet give him his way and he was always a most entertaining companion'.[1]

Lyte did not find Dr Maxwell's second wife easy to get on with. In a letter sent to Anne at the Maxwells' home (22 Bennett Street, Bath), Lyte wrote: 'Kind and affable as Mrs Maxwell is I could not feel comfortable in her society . . . I felt that my presence was an incumbrance.'[2] None the less when the stepmother died in 1847 she left the whole of her estate to Anne.[3]

[1] All the material in this paragraph is from Lyte's biography of Maxwell.
[2] An undated letter from the family papers, clearly written about 1818.
[3] Garland, *op. cit.,* p. 25.

4

AFTER THE MARRIAGE

THE MARRIAGE began happily, as it was to remain until the end. Lyte wrote to John Kerr at the time:[1]

'I was married at Bath on the 21st of January and immediately brought my dear wife down here, to my little residence at the end of the world where we have continued to live in happy retirement ever since, every day, I believe, mutually better pleased with our choice. My dear Anne is destitute of everything that is styled brilliant or striking. She is quiet, simple, plain and unassuming, full of tenderness and affection. Her taste is more for the playful, the elegant and the pathetic than for the bold, sublime and energetic. She does not want discernment and she thinks for herself, is fond of poetry, a great admirer of Cowper and speaks of your elegy as one of the most beautiful things she ever met with. The delicate intermingling of the heart and imagination which it exhibits, exactly suits her taste. Our sentiments on most subjects perfectly agree. We spend our mornings each in our respective employments, I at my desk or in my parochial engagements, and she in her kitchen or at her work. In the evenings we are always together and very happily and swiftly do they glide away in conversation or reading. We have the prospect, too, of having a family and affording another cousin to your little Helen.'

True to his word a son, Henry William Maxwell Lyte, was born on 29 September 1818 and baptised by his father at Marazion on Christmas Day. The family lived at Nevada House, a fairly large residence in Fore Street, the name of which has remained unchanged to this day.[2] From the back of the house there are beautiful views of the sea crowned by St Michael's Mount, which must have reminded Lyte of its elder sister Mont S Michel that he had seen on his horseback tour.

Very soon after his marriage Lyte began researching into his ancestry. He knew that he came from an old Somerset family and had married

[1] This unabridged version can only be seen, as far as we know, in the draft notes for Walter Maxwell-Lyte's book. The original letter has apparently been lost.
[2] T. Reynolds, Local Historian, Penzance, letter to the author, 23.6.1971.

into a family connected with the peerage. He naturally wished to be able
to tell his bride something about his ancestry. As far as he knew he was
an orphan and his only relative apart from his brothers was Captain
Thomas Lyte who claimed to be his uncle. So he wrote various letters
enquiring about his origins. Amongst the family papers is a letter from
the Rev. R. Lundie, Parish Minister of Kelso, written on 29 April 1818,
the very day on which Captain Lyte and his five-year-old daughter Harriet
arrived for their three-month stay with the Lytes at Marazion. This
letter was in reply to one from H. F. Lyte on 4 April which he had
addressed to a Mr Mason, who he had thought was the Postmaster at
Kelso. Lyte's letter evidently asked Mason if there were any records of
his family in the church registers at Kelso and Ednam. Mr Lundie replied
that the baptisms of both Lyte and his younger brother George were
recorded in the Ednam Baptism Registers. He enclosed copies of the two
entries signed by James Riddell, Session Clerk, dated 17 April 1818.
Lyte's own entry reads: 'Thomas Lyte Esqr residing at Ednam, and Anna
Maria Lyte his spouse, had a Son Baptised 13th June 1793 named Henry
Francis.' His brother's entry is precisely similar, apart from name and
date. Mr Lundie mentioned that he himself had been acquainted with
H. F. Lyte's father and mother for many years, and he asked how and
where Captain Lyte was. He added that one of the Lyte boys was a
great favourite of his, but he could not remember which.

Another letter was written very soon afterwards by James Ballantyne
of Edinburgh, a noted Scottish lawyer who is still remembered as the
publisher of Sir Walter Scott's novels. Evidently Lundie had told him
of his recent correspondence with Lyte, and Ballantyne wrote quite
spontaneously to the latter:

'I cannot resist the impulse which leads me to enquire after your
parents. While Mr and Mrs Lyte lived in Kelso and its neighbourhood, my family was in habits of closest intimacy with them . . .
I have myself carried you and your brother very often in my arms.
For nearly twenty years we have been in compleat ignorance of the
residence of your parents, and even whether they existed or not . . .
May I then, sir, request that you will have the goodness to relieve
my earnest desire to know where Mr Lyte now is, and in what
situation? Your mother, I think is no longer in existence. (Ballantyne
was apparently incorrect in this assumption). If you will, at the
same time, have the goodness to give me any particulars about my
little rosy friend, Henry Francis Lyte, who loved me very dearly

twenty years ago, it will be extremely gratifying to me. You have lived too short a time to be yet aware, how very tenderly and wistfully the friends of their youth are regarded by those who have reached the middle of life.'

Lyte evidently wrote back, and received a further letter from Ballantyne dated 3 September 1818:

'I will not conceal from you, that I have reason to think your parents were never married in the form which constitutes a legal union, in the Church, and by the law, of England; but I am very sure they resided in Scotland in circumstances which constituted a lawful marriage by the law of that country. Mr Thomas Lyte introduced Mrs Lyte, your mother, to the most respectable families in Roxburghshire, as his wife; his children were entered in a bible, which I have seen, as the children of "Thomas and Maria Lyte" and my friend Mr Lundie, the clergyman of Kelso, informs me, that your own name, if I mistake not, and that of a younger brother, whom you do not mention—George Lyte—were entered in the parish register of Ednam, as the children—of course the lawful children—of Thomas and Maria Lyte. The inference I draw from these particulars, in the first place, is, that, however their union originated, it was the purpose of both your parents to constitute a marriage, in that manner which was effectual, and which they knew to be effectual, in the country where they resided for many years; and, in the second place, that, even supposing such *not* to have been their intention, the mutual acknowledgements which they made, both in the ceremonies of baptism, and in their uniform intercourse with society, would have constituted a marriage by the law of the country, as it certainly did in the society in which they moved, whether they intended it or not. Had they continued to reside in Scotland, I have no manner of doubt, that every result of the marriage tie would have been as imperative upon them during their mutual lives, and as effectual to their children after their deaths, as if they had been united in the most formal manner, by a regular clergyman, and after proclamation of banns. But I do not know, and, what is extremely singular, I have not been able to learn, what are the effects of such an informal marriage, either with respect to the parents or their children, when the parents remove forth from Scotland to another country. It will, however, be some satisfaction to you to be assured, that so completely were your parents regarded as persons honourably and legally married, while in Scotland, that their intercourse was cultivated by several of the very first families, in point of rank and wealth, in Roxburgh and Berwickshire; as well as by numerous others in a lower, but still most reputable rank in life. In these counties indeed, such an avowal as Mr Thomas Lyte has made to you, his son, would warrant and incite very general indignation.'

Ballantyne, in this long letter, goes on to say that no good effect would be likely to result from any attempt by Lyte to force his father to acknowledge the legitimacy of his first marriage. He continues:

'But in the most earnest manner I would adjure you, by every motive of humanity, prudence, and good sense, to conceal all this painful detail from the pure ears of your wife. Had you married her under the load of a secret which you thought a discreditable one then certainly you would have been to blame. But you did not. You offered her *yourself;* and I can see nothing but cruelty in forcing upon her knowledge a painful and miserable history, which did not reach your ears until your fate had been irrevocably linked with hers. No, sir. That history it seems to me not pardonable in you, but bounden upon you, to bury in oblivion; and should any unhappy chance bring it to light, still your motives in the concealment must appear honourable and virtuous. Might I be permitted to give another opinion, though certainly with much less decision, I should think it better you were not acknowledged by your father at all than under a relation which you do not actually bear to him.'

This letter speaks for itself and it hardly becomes a writer with no legal qualifications to do more than point out that whether or not H. F. Lyte was legitimate is a very academic question after such a long passage of time. To Lyte it was obviously important since there was the question whether he and his two brothers or the issue of Eliza Naghten were the legitimate descendants of Captain Thomas Lyte. It will be remembered that Captain Lyte and his infant daughter by the 'second' marriage, Harriet, had stayed with the Lyte family for three months from 29 April 1818. No doubt Lyte had invited his 'uncle' over to find out more about his ancestry, and being confronted with the stark facts by Thomas Lyte almost immediately on the latter's arrival, he had taken the opportunity to consult Ballantyne, who had chanced to write at the vital moment.

Evidently H. F. Lyte did not reveal to his wife immediately the secret of his parentage, for he still described Thomas Lyte as his uncle in a letter he wrote to Mrs Lyte on 12 September 1818 from Bath, where he was helping to settle up his father-in-law's estate. The letter mentioned that Dr Maxwell's relatives 'did not chuse' to invite Thomas Lyte to the funeral! Whether H. F. Lyte disclosed the secret to his wife in later years is uncertain. Lyte was in correspondence with his father as late as 1837, however, so the secret may well have come out.[1] Two further letters written by Lyte later in 1818, one to the Headmaster of Portora and one to Mrs Williams of Ballyshannon, both presumably enquiring as to the whereabouts of Lyte's mother, brought replies on 24 and 28 December 1818 respectively, but neither correspondent was able to give any useful information.

The second matter which took up much of Lyte's time just after his marriage was the settlement of his father-in-law's estate. On 4 September 1818, three weeks before his first grandchild Henry was born, Dr Maxwell passed away at the age of eighty-five and was buried at Walcot Chapel where his daughter had been married. 'He died in the most calm and placid manner', Lyte tells us in his biography, 'His faculties seemed to be worn out and he sunk off as it were into a sweet slumber'. In the same document Lyte records that Dr Maxwell left a considerable sum of money, apart from his Irish estate at Falkland. The house there had been allowed to fall into ruin during Dr Maxwell's old age, and a tenant cut the timber and damaged the property in the landlord's absence. After leaving an annuity of £1,000 to the widow and a further £1,000 p.a. for the maintenance of his retarded son, Dr Maxwell left the residue of his estate in the hands of trustees for the benefit of his son and his heirs, should he recover the use of his intellect. Handsome bequests were also made to various other relatives, friends and servants, and a sum was left to educate poor children at Donagh.[2]

Lyte evidently travelled to Bath within a day or two of his father-in-law's death, and three letters written from there by him to his wife at Marazion still survive. The first, written on 9 September, is very affectionate in its tone. 'We have read the Will—our share is £400 a year' he declares, explaining that most of the money was left to Mrs Maxwell and her stepson. In the same letter he says his health was 'perfect', but he was consulting Dr Fox. A second letter written three days later states that

[1] A letter written by Lyte to his daughter late in 1837 mentions that he would have to visit 'the old Captain' at Christchurch.

[2] This last item comes from the article on Maxwell in the *Dictionary of National Biography,* all the rest from Lyte's biography of Maxwell.

their share of the estate, according to Watts the solicitor, might only be
£330 p.a. after all! A third letter, undated but clearly written at about
the same time, says that Dr Maxwell executed a codicil to his will
raising the Lytes' income from the estate to £600 a year, but that the
codicil was never signed and was therefore null and void. He mentions
that he had seen Dr Fox who confirmed that he was perfectly well:
'never mind physic or physicians until you need them.'

The Lytes must have had considerable anxiety about the disposition of
Dr Maxwell's estate, Mrs Lyte having been used to the very good standard
of living at her father's house, while her husband largely depended for his
income on the 'meagre pew rents'. We have found no record of Lyte's
stipend while at Marazion, apart from the £100 p.a. he received from
the neighbouring parish of Perranuthnoe. His Licence to the later
curacy at Charleton states that his salary there was £80 p.a. During his
incumbency of Lower Brixham his stipend was initially £80 and later
£134 p.a., no parsonage house being provided! Garland, page 24,
records that Dr Maxwell had allowed the Lytes £200 p.a. immediately
on their marriage, which had been doubled to £400 after his death.

The mentally retarded John Maxwell lived on until after Lyte's
decease but was never cured of his mental deficiency. The Will provided
that in the event of John Maxwell's death the landed property of the
estate passed first to Anne and then to her eldest son, while the residue of
the funded property passed to the Lytes' younger children in common.
While we have not been able to discover all the details it is clear that
Mrs Lyte and her family obtained considerable sums from the estate,
despite the restriction concerning John Maxwell. Lyte's correspondence
from Rome with his wife in February 1847 mentions a Chancery Court
action over the will and a letter written by him in October 1846 mentions
a substantial sum of money coming as 'Mrs Maxwell's gift'. There may
have been earlier court proceedings over the will, on the grounds that
John Maxwell was never likely to be able to use the money. Even
allowing for the extra income Lyte earned from his teaching, one could
not account for his high income in the mid-thirties and early forties, or
for the Lytes' ability to repay the cost of his education to Dr Burrowes[1]
unless they received substantial sums from the Maxwell family or Dr
Maxwell's estate. Towards the end of Lyte's life they were short of
money, the expense of his long spells on the Continent coupled with the

[1] W. Maxwell-Lyte, *British Weekly*, 3.4.1947, states that Lyte repaid his school
and university fees in full.

considerable cost of running Berry Head and its library and the cost of an Oxford or Cambridge education for all three sons being almost more than they could manage.

While at Marazion, though some weeks after he had resigned his curacy there, Lyte was invited to preach at a Bible Society service at St Mary's Chapel, Penzance on 28 November 1819. By request the text of the sermon was published as a pamphlet,[1] a copy of which is to be found amongst the Lyte family papers. The text was 'Search the Scriptures' (John 5, v. 39) and the sermon ran to thirty-six octavo pages of letterpress. It is notable in the first place for its Conservative Evangelical theology. There is virtually no reference to any doctrine of the Church, and Lyte seems to believe that a man can gain salvation simply by reading the Bible, praying and trying 'to do what the book says'. The preacher appears to hold a somewhat magical doctrine of biblical inspiration, since he claims that under the influence of the Spirit apparently meaningless passages became 'full of life and intelligence'. Lyte here teaches a rather extreme doctrine of the Fall of man similar to Calvin; man is corrupt and cannot learn about God from nature. He is here far removed from Aquinas who stressed that man was made in God's image.

The most striking feature of the sermon, however, is the political note on which it ends. Lyte feared a revolt from the poor (who he admitted were going through grievous suffering) in England on the lines of the French Revolution, and advised that the safest way to avert such a tragedy was to distribute the Bible! 'Never is disaffection more dangerous, especially among the lower orders, than when it takes irreligion for its ally . . . Let the multitude be once loosed from the restraints of religion, and all other restraints will soon be of little avail. Our own fears then, if not our sympathies, call upon us to supply the proper antidote to the poison that is spreading.' In a footnote to the sermon Lyte adds: 'It may not be from the purpose to add to what has been said above, that the Bible Society receives the countenance and support of almost every one of His Majesty's Ministers'.

It might surprise many younger Christians that Lyte, so noted for his care of poor fishermen, could speak of the 'lower orders' of society in this way, or say as he did that the poor, when bereft of all earthly support, would still find a God to pity them and a heaven to receive them. But here Lyte was a child of his times. He was a lifelong Conservative,

[1] Bristol 1820, printed for J. & W. Richardson, Clare-St. A fairly full summary is given in the author's MA thesis, Exeter University, 1973.

inheriting all the elegance of a county family who had dwelt for 500 years in their country mansion. He had an immense natural reverence for the Constitution and for law and order; indeed the very high value he put on the latter must have been an important factor behind his later acceptance of moderate Tractarian views. Like most human beings who do not suffer dire poverty or oppression in their youth, Lyte assumed that the social values of his formative years were largely sound, and he felt that the upper and lower classes were part of the natural order of society in a way which must seem strange to our present generation.

One need hardly add that the sermon is written in beautiful and most moving English prose, and, aided by Lyte's great natural gift for oratory it must have given powerful support to the Bible Society's plan to distribute the Scriptures far and wide. Even in those days, it seems from the sermon, many Christians were averse to the handing out of Bibles to those not necessarily in touch with any church, an attitude which Lyte found hard to understand.

By now Lyte's brief sojourn in Marazion was rapidly drawing to its end. The moist Cornish climate did not suit him, added to which the heavy programme of his marriage, the birth of his first child and the settlement of his father-in-law's estate, all occurring in the same year, must have strained his health considerably. On medical advice the family decided to move to the drier climate of the New Forest and left for Sway, Hampshire at the beginning of 1820 to live for a while in temporary retirement. While his curacy at Marazion officially terminated on 4 October 1819, his last baptism at the church was on 25 December the same year.

5

THE YEARS BEFORE BRIXHAM

S W A Y is a delightful village in the New Forest, some four miles from Lymington. Sway Cottage, where the Lytes lived from the beginning of 1820 until early in 1822, has been twice enlarged since their time, and is now known as Sway Place, a commodious residence in thirty-five acres of wooded grounds. Some years ago it was called 'The Hollies'; there seems to be no doubt as to the identity of the house, which is accepted by local historians.[1] Both Walter Maxwell-Lyte and Garland visited it about 1946. The former in a letter[2] writes: 'There has however been little alteration to the ancient part of the house, and the old pump, from which Lyte got his drinking water is still in use. We can also see the baking oven embedded in the brickwork in which Mrs Lyte used to bake her bread.' Garland reports similarly, and we ourselves found the pump and oven still there in 1971. In 1820 Sway Cottage was a small red-brick cottage. This part is intact, but it has been greatly enlarged by building on a much bigger wing, in matching red brick, at right angles to the old part. A local rate book dated 1820 does not mention Lyte as an householder; possibly he rented the cottage. According to an 1859 Directory Sway Cottage was then occupied by Mrs Lys, who owned much land in the area, so even then it must have been an important residence.[1]

In one or two places,[3] it is stated that Lyte held the curacy of Lymington, but the Winchester Diocesan Archivist can find no record of this,[4] nor can the Vicars of Lymington and Boldre (Sway Cottage then being in the latter parish) find any entries signed by Lyte in their registers. The *Remains,* page xx, records that at Lymington he enjoyed fuller leisure in quiet country life and that here he wrote a large part of his poems. Garland and Appleyard agree on this and it seems certain that

[1] Correspondence, 1971, between Edward King, Local Historian, Lymington and the author.
[2] Letter from W. Maxwell-Lyte, ca. 1947, in possession of Mrs Webber, Bramble Tor.
[3] e.g. *Dictionary of National Biography,* Vol. XII, p. 365.
[4] Letter from C. R. Davey, Deputy County Archivist of Hampshire, to the author, 14.11.72.

Lyte held no full-time post while at Sway and Dittisham. Many of his manuscript poems date from this period, and while at Sway Lyte wrote *Tales in Verse,* which was published later in 1826 and ran to two editions. Lyte's first printed book, it is dedicated to Mrs Yarde-Buller (Lady of the Manor at Brixham) and includes an open letter thanking her for the various acts of courtesy and kindness he had received from her and her husband. It is composed of six stories in verse, each one of which illustrates a clause of the Lord's Prayer. The plots of these very human stories would have done credit to Somerset Maugham. In the Preface Lyte apologises for the last story 'The Preacher' (illustrating 'Lead us not into temptation but deliver us from evil') in case it might appear to cast discredit on dissenting ministers. It is about a very gifted Nonconformist minister called Jones, who soon falls from his original devotion to God when the great acclaim given to his ministry leads him to become a pleaser of men. He then falls prey to the young niece of his landlady, and being pursued by her when she finds she is pregnant by him, he pushes her over a cliff. He is agonised by his conscience but continues to preach. Finally:

> And forth at last,
> In one strong groan his soul to judgement passed.

Wilson, reviewing this book in Blackwood's Magazine,[1] described it as 'the right kind of religious poetry'. Lyte's first book of poems as such, *Poems, Chiefly Religious,* was not published until 1833 and mention of this will be made later. Much of the material in *Poems, Chiefly Religious* and some of that in *The Spirit of the Psalms,* Lyte's metrical Psalter published in 1834, was however written while the family were at Sway and Dittisham.

The natural beauty of the New Forest, with its acres of countryside varying from rich forest to open moor and heathland, its noted flora and the charm of the wild ponies, provided a fertile ground for Lyte's poetic gift. One can imagine him strolling on foot, or riding on horseback, through the woods and fields and glades, very much as he had walked along the shores of Lough Erne or in the nearby woods in years gone past, sometimes composing poems in his thoughts, sometimes actually writing down the verses in his notebook as he walked along peaceful secluded woodland paths.

Garland, page 29, states that Lyte received his Dublin MA degree during the period at Sway; the same is stated in Walter Maxwell-Lyte's

[1] *Blackwood's Magazine,* Noctes Ambrosianae, No. 165, p. 686.

notes. According to Trinity College, Dublin,[1] however, it was in 1830 that Lyte was awarded his MA. It seems that the latter date is correct, since he is described as 'Bachelor of Arts' in his 1826 Deed of Institution to Lower Brixham Benefice, whereas the Address sent to him by the people of Brixham begging him not to leave for Penzance, and *The Spirit of the Psalms* (1834), both describe him as 'The Rev. H. F. Lyte, AM'. Lyte's entry in *Alumni Oxonienses* also gives the date of the Dublin MA as 1830, and it seems that the erroneous date came from the paragraph on Lyte in J. B. Leslie's *Ferns Clergy and Parishes,* published in 1936.

Garland states that Lyte travelled to Dublin to receive his MA while resident at Sway. Whether he travelled to Ireland for another purpose about 1820 is open to conjecture; the evidence is conflicting. According to the tradition in the Le Hunte family[2] Lyte attended the death-bed of his friend William Augustus Le Hunte at Wexford in February 1820. On the other hand Walter Maxwell-Lyte quotes H. F. Lyte as saying at the Protestant Meeting at Newton Abbot on 5 November 1828: 'I paid a visit to Ireland about two years ago after 10 or 12 years' absence from that country', which he uses as evidence that Lyte never visited Ireland in 1820.[3] He mentions the letter Lyte wrote to his wife from Drogheda on 19 September 1825 which must have been, he says, the visit of 'about two years ago'. In fact Lyte's Dublin *BA* certificate is dated 5 December 1827, although it notes that the degree was conferred on 2 February 1814.

In January 1821 the Lytes' first daughter Ann Maria Maxwell Lyte[4] was born at Sway Cottage and tragically died a month later. The Lytes had been delighted with the child, as Lyte's poem 'A.M.M.L.'[5] shows. On the manuscript copy of the poem Lyte wrote: 'Inscription for the grave of my dear little one Anna Maria who died at Sway Cottage, February 1821 aged 1 month'. The first two verses read:

> A few brief moons the Babe who slumbers here
> Smiled on her parents, and that innocent smile
> Was daylight to their eyes. They thought her fair,
> And gentle, and intelligent, and dared
> To lean their hearts upon her. There are ways
> And looks of hers that long will dwell with them,

[1] Letter from Trinity College, Dublin, Information Office, to the author, 17.11.1971.
[2] See below, page 132.
[3] *Belfast Newsletter,* 27.12.1947.
[4] So she is named in the Boldre Burial Register, but it is likely that 'Ann' was a mistake; the other relatives are all called Anna Maria.
[5] *Remains,* p. 205.

And there are bright anticipations held,
How fondly and feelingly resign'd!
Her very helplessness endear'd her to them,
And made her more their own—But this is done:—
The wintry wind pass'd o'er the opening flower,
And nipp'd it in the bud—and it is gone.

Still there is comfort left. It still is joy
That they can lift their weeping eyes to Heaven
And think that one of theirs is settled there;
Can know, beyond the shadow of a doubt,
That she is safe with Him who bears the lambs
Within His bosom, and, no longer Babe
But Angel, now beholds her Father's face,
And shares the fullness of eternal joy.

Her burial is duly recorded in the registers of Boldre Church, two and
a half miles from Sway Cottage; she was buried on 11 February 1821
by the Rev. C. Shrubb, Vicar, her address being given as North Sway.
In 1946 (approx.) Walter Maxwell-Lyte made an extensive search for her
grave without success, nor were we able to find the place of her burial
in the beautifully kept churchyard. The present Vicar of Boldre, the
Rev. J. C. E. Hayter, had no idea of this connection with the Lyte family
until we were able to point out the burial entry. There is no record of
Anna Maria's baptism there.

After two years at Sway Lyte was beginning to feel much better and
was obviously looking forward to the day when he would resume an
active ministry. So the family decided to move to the West Country once
more. Perhaps Lyte preferred to minister in that part of the world, or
possibly he had more friends in those parts who would help to find him a
parish. So early in 1822, when Lyte was twenty-eight, the family took a
large house called Bramble Torr, half a mile from Dittisham, Devon.
In those days Marazion was in Exeter Diocese, so Lyte was returning to his
old diocese, apparently not heeding any risk to his health which might
be incurred through the damper climate of the West.

The Lytes seemed to have a knack of selecting delightful spots for their
home (with the exception, perhaps, of their first house in Brixham) and
this could certainly be said of Dittisham. It is even to-day a very pretty
village, on the shores of the River Dart, which is nearly half a mile wide
at this point. The Dart Estuary from Dittisham to Dartmouth is nowadays
one of the best-patronised beauty spots in South Devon and in summer
pleasure boats and steamers continually ply the four miles of water

between Dittisham and the sea. The wider parts of the Dart, with the richly wooded hills in the background, look for all the world like an Austrian lake.

Bramble Torr (or Bramble Tor, as it is spelt to-day) has been a farm-house for many years and has been farmed by the Webber family ever since 1923. The house was originally built in 1767 and, despite more recent modifications at the back and side, the square grey frontage with a Monkey Puzzle tree in the garden has changed very little in appearance, apart from the size of the tree, since Lyte's time. Like most of the Lytes' houses it has always been large. Even to-day it is in the quietest of sur-roundings with green fields on every side.

The first important event after their arrival at Dittisham was the birth of their second (and only surviving) daughter on 20 April 1822 at Bramble Torr. Like her sister who had so sadly died she was named Anna Maria Maxwell Lyte. Even the second Anna Maria must have been weakly at birth, for the Dittisham Church registers record that she was 'baptized privately April 23rd publickly August 18th' by Lyte himself. Despite her frailty at birth she was to live to the age of sixty-seven.

It seems that at Dittisham, as at Sway, Lyte held no full-time post. We found no Licence of any kind granted to him at this time among the Exeter Diocesan records. During the early part of 1822 while at Bramble Torr, however, Lyte was asked to do temporary duty at the Chapel-of-Ease at Lower Brixham which was later to become his beloved parish church. Brixham was some five miles from Dittisham, on the opposite side of the Dart. An amusing tale told in Dittisham relates that Lyte used to ride a horse right through the river, which is of considerable depth at this point, and continue to Brixham on reaching the other side! Much more likely to be true is another version, found in a hand-written note on the back of a picture postcard in the possession of the Lyte family, to the effect that Lyte first crossed the Dart on the ferry and then proceeded to Brixham on horseback to conduct divine service at the Chapel.

The result of this was that as early as 31 May 1822 Lyte received a letter signed by William King, Chairman, and three other Trustees of the Lower Brixham Chapel, plus 146 members of the congregation, begging him to become their permanent Minister. In the letter those signing 'beg leave to offer you our most grateful acknowledgements for the superior manner in which the service has been performed—Tho' our experience of you has been but short, and we are led to apprehend that the period unhappily of your engagement may terminate in a few weeks . . . yet in

truth, Sir, we feel a controlling and something like an affectionate
Impatience to express to you without loss of time the earnest prepossession
of our minds—with a hope (we will not disguise it) of prevailing on you
to entertain the thought of settling among us permanently . . . Should
you feel yourself at liberty under any consideration that may satisfy
your own mind to become a candidate of our Chapel we present it to you
with willing hearts and if you come among us, we pledge ourselves to
contribute everything within our humble means to render your abode
comfortable and respected.'[1] The signatories include many names (such
as Hellier, Jordain, Silly, Furneaux, Rennels, Gillard and Pomeroy) still
very familar in the town, where there has been a great deal of inter-
marriage.

In the event Lyte did not accept the offer at this stage. The Trustees'
Minutes[2] noted that only the difficulty of finding a house made it out of
Lyte's power to continue his work at Lower Brixham Chapel; he himself
expressed 'a willingness to comply with such wish at some future time'.
One wonders in fact whether he had already all but agreed to go to
Charleton when this petition arrived, for he was actually licensed to the
curacy there on 6 July 1822, only six weeks later. At any rate to Charleton
he went, where he took charge of the parish for the absentee Rector the
Rev. George Smith.

Charleton was a scattered parish of some 500 souls about two miles
from Kingsbridge. The village is even to-day quite small, and the
charming little thirteenth-century church (extensively restored in 1850)
is set in the midst of rolling green fields. A half a mile away, and visible
from some parts of the village, is the Kingsbridge Estuary with its
picturesque 'lakeside' scenery. Three miles down the estuary is Salcombe
with its harbour and innumerable pleasure boats. In the early nineteenth
century up to 150 sailing ships from Charleton engaged in trade with the
Mediterranean ports.[3] Apart from the one exception of Sway, itself only
five miles from the sea, the Lyte family always managed to live in
riverside or seaside surroundings; after his early days on the shores of
Lough Erne Lyte probably found it difficult to live away from the waters
which were such a delight to him.

While at Charleton the Lytes lived at The Parsonage, as shown on

[1] From the Lyte family papers.
[2] The Minute Book having been lost, these Minutes are only known as quotes in
   The Story of All Saints', Brixham, a pamphlet by the then Vicar, W. A. Earp,
   published in 1946 by the British Publishing Company, Ltd., Gloucester.
[3] Garland, *op. cit.,* p. 31.

Lyte's Curate's Licence, signed by Bishop William Carey. His first recorded duty at Charleton was a burial on 14 August 1822, his last a funeral on 20 April 1824. His predecessor's last duty, a baptism, had been on 21 July 1822; his successor took a baptism before Lyte left on 18 April 1824. Charleton Parsonage is known to-day as Charleton Grange and is the home of a veterinary surgeon. The house is reputed to be 400 years old. It is a large rambling grey building set apart from the village in a secluded valley, with fine views of the estuary on the right-hand side. Externally it still looks very much as it must have done in Lyte's time. It ceased to be the Rectory about 1939.

We know little of Lyte's ministry in the village; Garland says that his services were well-attended. The Earl of Morley, who owned much property at Charleton and knew Lyte well,[1] wrote in 1835 in his testimonial letter to Lyte when the latter was seeking appointment as Vicar of Crediton: 'I perfectly recollect you having served the parish of Charleton to the entire satisfaction of the parishioners and I equally remember you having preached in our chapel at Saltram in the presence of the late Mr Canning a sermon, of which he ever afterwards spoke (and he did so frequently) in terms of the highest admiration.' There is no memorial to Lyte in the church.

It was this sermon, in the chapel in the grounds of Saltram House, the eighteenth-century stately home near Plymouth which was the Earl of Morley's family seat, which was to change the whole course of Lyte's life. George Canning and the Earl were close friends; Morley's illegitimate son Augustus Stapleton was later Canning's personal private secretary and wrote the stateman's biography after his death.[2] The sermon was preached on 19 October 1823 with Canning, who was then Foreign Secretary, in the congregation. Canning was so impressed that he discussed the sermon with Lyte after the service and asked for a copy of it, which was later sent. Canning was destined to be Prime Minister for four months in 1827 before his untimely death on 8 August that year.

Fortunately the text of this sermon, which was on the last five words of Ephesians 2, v. 12, 'Without God in the world,' has been preserved for us in the *Remains*.[3] In it Lyte compared the fate, in life and particularly in

[1] P. H. Dawes, Curator of Saltram House, letter to the author, 19.12.1972.
[2] P. H. Dawes, *loc. cit.*
[3] *Remains*, pp. 209f. The Sermon was preached again at Lower Brixham District Church on 5.3.1826 and published in the latter year as a 24-page pamphlet, dedicated to Canning, in aid of the enlargement of the church. This was printed by Messrs. Elburton & Henderson, Gough Street, London.

the face of approaching death, of a man who lived for God as against a man without God in the world. The sermon, like many of Lyte's addresses, shows a prominent 'hell-fire' note and was true to the tradition of Wesley and the Evangelical Revival. Yet there is a peculiar beauty about both the language and the content of the address. As with the Bible Society sermon at Penzance there is virtually no reference at all to the Church as an instrument of God, but there are signs of a slightly greater tolerance now, and in this address Lyte is not so sweeping in his condemnation of natural religion.

The result of this sermon before Canning is related in a letter from the Hon. Dudley Ryder to his brother Viscount Sandon (afterwards Earl of Harrowby), quoted by Walter Maxwell-Lyte:[1]

'I cannot resist sending you a sermon which was preached before poor Canning at Saltram in 1823 by Mr Lyte, the clergyman of Brixham, who has been the means of procuring a moral regeneration in that parish, the care of which was procured for him by Canning in consequence of his having heard this sermon, and has had several conversations with Mr Lyte after he had preached it. It is, in itself, an excellent sermon, of a high order in point of matter and composition—but it derives peculiar interest from having engaged Mr Canning's attention and approbation so strongly as to beg the author to lend it to him that he might read it to his family and talk over its contents with candour and freedom . . . Canning, ever after, showed the regard he entertained for Mr Lyte and got him the living of Brixham, as a substantial proof of it. He begged Mr Lyte to call upon him without fail when he came to London. But Mr Lyte, from Christian motives, did not do so when he was there. Canning met him by accident in the street and reproached him with every argument that sincere esteem could have dictated.

I mentioned this as very creditable to both parties, for Lyte had not scrupled to speak as a faithful expositor of Biblical truth in his conversation with Canning and this usually offends.'

About April 1824, therefore, Lyte left Charleton to begin his life's most important work at Brixham.

[1] *British Weekly,* 3.4.1947.

6

INTRODUCTION TO BRIXHAM

WHAT KIND of a town was it in which Lyte was now called to minister? Brixham is set in a delightful position at the southern extremity of Tor Bay, with magnificent views across the bay to Torquay four miles away and to distant cliffs beyond. On the eastern side it is bounded by the fine promontory of Berry Head just over a mile away; here the windswept cliffs rise to a height of 200 feet. Tor Bay has always been used as a natural harbour, although the small sailing ships of Lyte's time were never safe from easterly gales until the large breakwater was completed in 1916. Sea tragedies were commonplace, both in Lyte's day and for many years afterwards.

Brixham was an ancient settlement. Neolithic flints and Bronze Age remains have been found in the area, also a number of Roman coins. A great rampart on Berry Head was probably used as a Roman fort.[1] Later came a Saxon settlement which was at Higher Brixham, a mile inland. The Saxons were possibly colonists arriving by sea in the seventh century.[2] About the ninth century a Saxon church was built at Higher Brixham on the site of the present fifteenth-century Church of St Mary, which was the ancient parish church of the town. Brixham is mentioned in the Domesday Book,[3] where it is written 'Juhel has a manor called Briseham, which Ulf held on the day on which king Edward was alive and dead.'

Until the eighteenth century Brixham was a large inland village centred on St Mary's Church. The harbour, which was over a mile down the valley, was surrounded by green meadows and hills, only a handful of houses being clustered on either side of the harbour, close to the water. The main industry of Brixham was then agriculture, although even by the sixteenth century there must have been a fair amount of fishing, as in the 1535 *Valor Ecclesiasticus* the fish tithe for Brixham was £17, compared with £12 each for Torquay and Paignton, £6 for

[1] Information supplied by Mr C. H. Rock, Curator of Brixham Museum.
[2] J. R. Pike, *Brixham: Torbay* (pamphlet), 1973, p. 2.
[3] Exch. D. 109 (i); 19a, quoted *Devonshire Domesday*, 1884–92, p. 595.

Dawlish, £4 for Seaton and £3 for Clovelly.[1] The other Brixham tithes
that year were: Wool and Lambs £11. 13s. 4d., Veal, Appels and
Offering £23.[2] As in those days most clergy livings were £8–£10 p.a.
we might regard a £17 tithe as worth £3,000 in present day (1973)
currency, suggesting that some £30,000 worth of fish would be landed in
a year even in 1535 (in 1973 it was £822,938). Leland called Brixham
'a praty town of fischar men' when he visited it in 1525.[3] W. G. Hoskins[4]
suggests that Brixham was Devon's No 1 port in 1535, and remained so
until overtaken by Plymouth in the 1870s.

Despite these sizeable catches of fish in earlier days, Lower Brixham
expanded out of all recognition from 1760 onwards. The meadows and
hills surrounding the harbour fast became covered with grey cottages
and houses. By 1801 the population of Brixham was 3,671 and in 1841 it
had reached 5,684,[5] as against the thousand or so souls living near St
Mary's Church who had made up almost the entire population of the
town up to the mid-eighteenth century. A good part of the expansion
was due to the fact that Torbay had become an important naval base
during the Napoleonic Wars, when the Channel Fleet was based on
Torbay and all the large vessels used Brixham as a watering station;
water was piped to the harbour-side from a reservoir on the site of the
present Town Hall, a quarter of a mile away.[6] It was thought necessary,
too, to place an Army garrison at Berry Head to protect the Fleet.

None the less, the main reason for this transformation of Lower
Brixham was the sudden development of the new, or rather revived,
method of fishing known as trawling. Brixham is justly known as the
'Mother of the Deep Sea Fisheries'. Up to this time fishing at Brixham
had been from the surface of the sea, by drift or moored nets, or by rod
and line. But now came in the trawl, a weighted net shaped like a great
open sack, which is dragged along the sea-bed behind its parent ship or
trawler. Trawling was practised at least as early as 1376, but in the
Middle Ages it was frowned upon, because it was believed to deplete the
stocks of fish. Even to-day British inshore fishermen are required by law
to use a fairly large mesh net, so that the smaller fish escape and stocks
are thereby preserved.

[1] V. C. Boyle and D. Payne, *Devon Harbours,* 1952, pp. 68–9.
[2] P. Varwell, *Transactions of the Devonshire Association,* 1886, Vol. XVIII, pp. 197f.
[3] Leland, III, 31.
[4] W. G. Hoskins, *A New Survey of England, Devon,* 1954, p. 349.
[5] Wm. White, *History, Gazetteer and Directory of Devonshire,* 1850, p. 188.
[6] E. R. Delderfield, *Torbay Story,* 1951, p. 14.

A second reason why trawling did not develop on any scale for centuries was that in order to drag the trawl along the sea-bed at an adequate speed (about one and a half knots) it was necessary to have a ship of such speed that *without* the trawl it could sail at about eight knots. But with the old three-mast square-sailed ship this would only have been possible in a near-gale when conditions for fishing would have been dangerous. In moderate or fresh winds these old ships were too slow to drag the trawl at an effective speed.[1]

In the mid-seventeenth century this problem was solved by the invention in Holland of the more modern 'fore and aft' rigging such as is used for sailing yachts to-day. With the new rigging a small two-mast trawler could sail at the requisite speed even in a moderate wind, and trawling now became a commercial possibility. Furthermore in about 1760 a new market for fish was set up through the great improvement of the turnpike roads. Fresh fish could now be taken by road from Brixham to Exeter and to an important market at Bath, where 'money flowed like water'. It was soon found that with the right mesh to the net there was no need to fear that the sea would be fished out by the trawlers.[1] Great quantities of turbot and sole, which had previously lain unmolested at the bottom of the sea, could now readily be caught. Good supplies of cod, hake, whiting, haddock and flat fish could also be taken by the trawl.[2]

The first to take up trawling on any scale were the fishermen of Barking on Thames-side. In spite of the official veto they maintained a fleet of 40 trawlers in the mid-seventeenth century. In time the Barking fishermen spread out and established trawling at Harwich, Yarmouth and elsewhere, but it was not until the Brixham fishermen took it up a century later that trawling was established on a national footing. This was perhaps due to the natural enterprise of the Devonians, who had produced Drake and Raleigh. The Brixham development may also have been due to the thousands of men returning from the Seven Years' War in 1763 bringing overseas ideas back with them.[3] The Brixham skippers, though often barely able to write, were always great seamen. The Brixham trawling was quite a separate development from that at Barking; the equipment differed in certain respects, and instead of being paid wages like the Barking men, the Brixham fishermen were each paid a percentage

[1] V. C. Boyle and D. Payne, *op. cit.,* pp. 72f.
[2] V. C. Boyle and D. Payne, *loc. cit.;* W. A. Saxton, *The Fishing Industry in Brixham,* pamphlet, 1970.
[3] Percy Russell, *Transactions of the Devonshire Association,* 1951, Vol. LXXXIII, p. 286.

or 'share' of the value of the catch, which was an added incentive to work hard. In the nineteenth century Brixham trawlermen established by colonisation the great trawler fleets at Grimsby and Hull, and their descendants founded the trawler port at Fleetwood on the west coast, so that they were virtually founders of the whole industry in Britain. It is said that the Brixham men were the first to discover the Dogger Bank fishing ground.[1]

From 1760 onwards, then, the old Brixham around St Mary's Church rapidly became dwarfed by the new town of Lower Brixham or Brixham Quay springing up around the harbour. By 1785 some seventy-five trawlers were operating from Brixham. Markets for the fish were now extended to London and Portsmouth. A Petition in 1799 resulted in an Act of Parliament in the same year authorising the building of a fish market and a second outer quay. By 1914 there were 350 trawlers in Brixham harbour.[2]

It was in this context that Lyte arrived in Brixham in the spring of 1824. One result of this sudden 'invasion' of mariners, many of whom came from other parts of the country, was that there was insufficient room at St Mary's Church for the greatly increased number of worshippers. Furthermore the long-established residents of old Brixham (mostly agricultural workers but including some of the old sea-going families) did not welcome the new arrivals living at 'The Quay'. Upper Brixham families did not allow their womenfolk to go down to the Quay, with some justification, as the morals of the new seafaring population were often open to considerable criticism. Even to-day a mild antipathy or rivalry exists between the two districts. However, as churchmen the Lower Brixham populace had to be tolerated at St Mary's, and the first step to find room for them had been the erection of the Quay Gallery (with an outside entrance and staircase!) at the old parish church in 1792.[3]

Very soon even this was inadequate to accommodate the new people, and with St Mary's being a good mile from the main population centre of the town the need for a church in Lower Brixham became acute. No church or chapel existed there until the Baptists came in 1801, fifteen years before any other denomination. To this day many Lower Brixham families describe themselves as Baptists, though quite often they are unbaptised.

[1] Sidney Heath, *The South Devon and Dorset Coast*, 1910, p. 100.
[2] Stanley R. Baron, *Westward Ho! From Cambria to Cornwall*, 1934, p. 213.
[3] *St Mary's Church, Brixham, Short History and Guide*, 4th edition, 1948. (Anonymous pamphlet, written originally by the Rev. F. J. S. Morris).

In 1813 a meeting was held at the London Inn, Brixham, with the Rev. Robert Holdsworth, Vicar of Brixham, in the chair. It was decided to build a Chapel near Brixham Quay, the money being raised by shares of £2. 13s. od., each shareholder being entitled to one sitting and one vote, on payment of a yearly rent.[1] Subscriptions were also invited, and Lysons states that £1,050 altogether was raised.[2] The Chapel was completed in 1816 and licensed for worship on 22 April that year by the Bishop of Exeter. The foundation stone had been laid on 24 June 1814 by Richard Lavers, Master of the Freemasons' Lodge. The Chapel was in the charge of Trustees who appointed (no doubt with the Vicar's consent) the minister.

The first priest-in-charge, the Rev. William Marshall, stayed until 1820 but after that the Trustees' Minutes record the appointment of a succession of ministers 'who either wished to leave after six months, or were asked to do so!'[3] Only two years after Marshall's departure Lyte had begun his temporary ministry at the chapel, and it is hardly surprising in view of this background that the Trustees were so anxious for him to stay. However, for the moment this was not to be.

The next step was to secure the endowment of the chapel and have it consecrated as a parish church. For this a grant of £1,200 was obtained from the Parliamentary Commissioners.[4] The Trustees now had to convey the chapel and land to His Majesty's Commissioners; this was effected in August 1823. In future the minister would not be appointed by the Trustees but would be nominated as Incumbent by the Crown.

On 9 September 1824 the church was duly consecrated by the Bishop of Exeter. The Consecration Deed, which is still stored at the Diocesan Registry and has a plan of the church attached, shows the church to have been a narrow rectangular building with a gallery, seating 600 in all. A newspaper article[5] stated that the District Church had lately been 'completed and enlarged', but the enlargement must have been very slight at this stage for the original chapel also seated 600, as stated in its Licence for Divine Worship. Like so many Anglican churches of its day its appearance was very similar to that of a Nonconformist chapel. The tiny holy table or altar was almost completely hidden by the central pulpit which

[1] T. Long, *The Story of All Saints' Church, Brixham,* pamphlet, 1933.
[2] Lysons, *Magna Britannia,* 1822, Vol. 6, Part 2, p. 72.
[3] W. A. Earp, *The Story of All Saints' Church, Brixham,* pamphlet, 1946.
[4] S. Lewis, *Topographical Dictionary of England,* 5th edition, 1842, Vol. I, p. 387.
[5] *Western Luminary,* Exeter, 14.9.1824. Lyte's name is not mentioned in the account.

dominated the interior. In front of the pulpit at a lower level was the minister's desk, and at a still lower level the clerk's desk, forming the 'three-decker' arrangement so familiar in those days. The pulpit has remained to this day, but it is now of course at the side.

Lyte probably arrived in Brixham soon after his last duty at Charleton in April 1824, for he was appointed to the Brixham National School Committee the next month.[1] His signature does not appear in the St Mary's Registers, however, until 18 October 1824, when he took a baptism. Lower Brixham Church had no registers of its own until it was fully constituted as a separate parish in 1826. Until then Lyte was tech-nically a curate of St Mary's, Brixham with charge of the new District Church of Lower Brixham. Although mainly concerned with the latter church, Lyte officiated at St Mary's as well between 1824 and 1826, and married a number of couples at St Mary's during that period. Before 1826 it is difficult to tell whether Lyte's baptisms were at the District Church or at St Mary's for they would have been registered at St Mary's in either case.

On 13 July 1826 Lyte was instituted by the Bishop of Exeter as the first incumbent of Lower Brixham, the necessary formalities involved in setting up the new parish having been completed. Lyte is always described in Brixham as the first Vicar of All Saints' Church, and for convenience we shall in future refer to Lower Brixham Church as All Saints'. In point of fact, however, the parish did not become a vicarage until 1866, well after Lyte's time.[2] Officially Lyte was never Vicar but Minister Incum-bent. Furthermore the title of All Saints' was not used until much later; it first appears in the Vestry Book in 1890 and the old title of the District Church of Lower Brixham was still used right up to 1920. For all practical purposes, however, Lyte was now Vicar of All Saints'; his first wedding there was on 16 July and the first baptism actually to be registered at All Saints' was on 23 July 1826.

For their first residence the Lytes rented Burton House in Burton Street, no parsonage house being provided until well after their time. The house, which has a pleasant Queen Anne exterior, has recently been modernised and converted into Burton Court flats; happily the old frontage has been retained. After the Lytes left it was for many years the doctor's house, the road facing it now being called Doctors Road. In the garden is a large weeping ash tree said to have been planted by Lyte. Behind the house

[1] Brixham National Schools—Managers' Minute Book.
[2] *London Gazette*, 3 April 1866, 2211.

could be seen 'until recent years', as Appleyard wrote in 1939,[1] a large rock which formed a picturesque object on a sloping bank. On the rock was fixed by Lyte's orders a tablet, now in Brixham Museum, bearing an epitaph he composed for a much-loved dog belonging to Lady Farnham: 'Here lies Var (Lapdog of the Right Honourable Lady Farnham)'—a verse by Lyte follows. Thus the stage was set for Lyte's twenty-three years' ministry in Brixham.

[1] J. Appleyard, *Henry Francis Lyte,* 1939, p. 28.

7

THE OPENING YEARS AT LOWER BRIXHAM

WHAT KIND of person was Lyte when he set out on his life's greatest task? We have seen that he was tall and unusually handsome, slightly eccentric but of great personal charm, a man noted for his wit and human understanding, a born poet and an able scholar. According to his great grandson John Maxwell-Lyte,[1] he was an expert flute player and always had his flute with him. His diaries show him to have had a warm and affectionate nature which must have been a great help in fostering human contacts. His daughter[2] tells us that his talents and personal attractions gained him a high position amongst his contemporaries and that his struggles in early life had given him 'an energy of purpose, and a vigorous determination to overcome all difficulties, which contrasted strangely with his natural gentleness of disposition, and calm enjoyment of intellectual pursuits— while his high classical attainments, which he pursued the more ardently from a keen perception of, and love for, their own beauty, imparted an almost Attic elegance of thought and diction, and gave a poetic colouring to his view of the most ordinary things of life. This he never lost'. Of his sermons Mrs Hogg wrote[3]: 'In his sermons too he rarely, if ever, preached precisely as he wrote . . . those who best remember his own peculiar flow of eloquence, and charm of voice and manner, will not fail, in glancing over the few sermons given in this volume, to feel how far short they fall of his own impressive and impassioned style, when wanting his voice to utter, and his mind to add its own grace and finish to the whole.' Allowing for his daughter's natural bias in his favour, one must add that if Lyte's spoken sermons were so much better than the written words, which themselves were often immensely telling and beautiful, they must have been brilliant indeed! Walter Maxwell-Lyte[4] adds that he was gentle, unassuming, stern when the occasion demanded it, patient under suffering, thoughtful for others, cultured and well-read, witty and amusing, a

[1] Letter to Walter Maxwell-Lyte, 19 August (1947?), Lyte family papers.
[2] *Remains,* pp. xii, xiii.
[3] *ibid.,* p. vii.
[4] *British Weekly,* 3.4.1947.

generous and kind host, so that 'it is easy to realise why he was loved by all who knew him'.

Another gift Lyte possessed, very much more fashionable to-day than it was 150 years ago, was the ability to identify himself with his flock. In the poem 'Grace Darling's Deathbed',[1] for example, he shows how much the hard life of a fisherman, with danger always just around the corner, had become part of himself, despite the gentlemanly society he so often enjoyed. A popular pamphlet on Lyte, which in a woodcut shows the minister walking around the harbour immaculately clad in top hat and tails, yet receiving a very friendly smile from two rough old fishermen whom many clergymen of those days would not have deigned to recognise, is very close to the mark. The *Remains,* page xxix, says that he used to visit fishermen on board their vessels in harbour, as well as in their homes, and supplied every vessel with a Bible. He compiled a brief manual of Devotions for their use while at sea, and also wrote some naval songs, adapting them to popular tunes.

On page xxii of the work, Mrs Hogg records that Lower Brixham did not attract the sympathy of a refined and highly-cultivated mind and that Lyte only went to 'so uncongenial a sphere' when it seemed to be the path of duty. Even so he never left Brixham and the town seemed to grow on him over the years. The *Remains* goes on to describe Brixham folk as shrewd and busy but uneducated people, rough but warm-hearted. There was much vice in the town, due in considerable measure to the large body of military and naval forces there, and this shed an influence most unfavourable to the growth of morality or religion. It was wise to put Lyte there as a pastor, Mrs Hogg adds, because he breathed another atmosphere from that which hung around his daily path.

One might have supposed that, never having worked in this type of parish before, Lyte might have spent a year or two finding his bearings before launching out on any far-reaching schemes. But this was not to be so. Even before he had become incumbent Lyte had made some notable advances, especially in the field of education. After a preliminary scheme based on the Methodist Meeting House had begun in 1816, two years later Brixham's National Schools had been built on the steeply sloping Windmill Hill site near the town centre. The building held 100 boys and 100 girls, and the idea was that all poor children from Brixham and nearby Churston should be educated there at very low cost—from June 1821

[1] *Remains,* p. 37.

each child paid ½d. a week—with the help of a local charity.[1] Brixham faced a special problem in that many boys went to sea at nine or ten destitute of education, so that if they had the ability to be pilots or skippers they had to give place to those of better education.

Soon after his arrival in Brixham Lyte was invited to join the Schools Committee, and by June 1824 he had become Chairman.[1] During his time Lyte often conducted the annual school examinations, which took place in public. In 1842, for example, the examination took place before a 'highly respectable audience'; the Rev. Mr Lyte examined the children on the Liturgy while the Vicar of Brixham, the Rev. Mr Holdsworth, examined them on the Catechism. 'The answering of the children was extremely satisfactory and the singing on the new system elicited general praise.' In 1840 Lyte had proposed that the children be instructed in 'the new plan of Musick'. This was the tonic sol-fa system, by no means new in fact but new to the school. The building had two schoolrooms (until enlarged in 1875) and the Master, Mr King, resided in a house adjoining them, for which he paid a rent. There was also a Mistress, Miss Cumming; both these teachers died in 1832.

This was just one example of Lyte's keenness for social reform, despite his lifelong Conservative politics. Appleyard, page 24, states that Lyte assisted the local MP, Sir John Yarde-Buller, with his schemes to improve national education. The rapid expansion of the industrial population over these years had made educational and social reforms a matter of high priority. Quite apart from the virtue of such reforms in themselves it was widely voiced, and in Lyte's Penzance sermon almost foreshadowed, that something akin to the French Revolution would happen in Britain if help was not soon brought to the suffering industrial masses.

More pioneering still, perhaps, was Lyte's work in the Sunday School field. Although there had been isolated instances of schools for the poor meeting on Sundays earlier on, it was Robert Raikes in 1780 who really founded the Sunday School movement in Britain when at Gloucester in co-operation with the local incumbent T. Stock, he engaged four women to teach the children reading and Church Catechism on Sundays. Unfortunately no detailed history of Sunday Schools has yet been written, and the National Christian Education Council (formerly the Sunday School Union) could not give us any information as to the number of Sunday Schools in England in Lyte's time. An Encyclopaedia article,[2]

[1] E. Littlechild, *The Passing of Brixham Girls' School,* pamphlet, 1963.
[2] W. C. R. Hicks, *Chambers Encyclopaedia,* 1967, Vol. 15, p. 284.

however, states that by 1787 Manchester alone had over forty Sunday Schools, which had spread to many towns in Britain by 1784. By 1789 it was estimated that 300,000 children in Britain were attending them, and Lyte mentions 'the little damsels of the sunday school' in his first story, 'Harford', in the *Tales in Verse*. As in many instances, however, the West of England was a little behind the rest of the country. Walter Maxwell-Lyte states[1] that in founding the Sunday School at Brixham in 1824 Lyte was the pioneer of Sunday Schools in the West Country. We would ourselves be inclined to think that there were Sunday Schools in Exeter by 1824, for by 1838 there were 2,470 Anglican and 1,193 Nonconformist children attending Sunday Schools in that city.[2] All local literature attests, however, that Lyte's Sunday School was the first in Torbay area.

Although religious instruction was always given in Sunday Schools, their main purpose in early days was to provide general education for children who worked such long hours in mills and factories that week-day schooling was virtually impossible for them. Lyte himself undertook work of this kind; in his Coronation Sermon to the fishermen in 1838 he mentioned that his Sailors' Sunday School offered to those who could not read the opportunity of learning to do so, and to those who could read the chance of having what they read explained to them. The fact that 200 children received week-day education at the National School, while between 800 and 1,000 attended Sunday School in Brixham, shows how advantageous Sunday education could be.

Even so, Lyte went much further than this; he turned his Sunday School into the attractive 'children's church' it often became up and down the country in later years. A great feature of his Sunday School was the Annual Treat. Still amongst the family papers is a hymn-sheet for the 'Twelfth Anniversary of the Brixham Sunday School Treat' held on Wednesday, 17 August 1836. It includes six hymns of the poet's own composition, a typical verse being:

> A little lowly band are we
> And Christ our heavenly King
> Yet Jesus deigns our Friend to be
> And hears us while we sing
> Halleluiah to the Lamb
> That died on Mount Calvary
> Halleluiah, Halleluiah, Halleluiah, Amen.
>
> (The last line a refrain).

---

[1] *The Life of Faith*, 12.11.1947.
[2] Robert Newton, *Victorian Exeter*, 1968, p. 218 (quotes Government returns).

The Treat began with a short service in church, at which in 1836 three hymns were sung. Then clergy, teachers and children went in procession to a field near Berry Head House where three more hymns were sung; afterwards there were tea and sports in the field. To the hundreds of poverty-stricken children this was indeed a tremendous treat. Even the singing of hymns was something of a novelty at the time and Lyte delighted the children by writing new hymns for the Treat every year. It is probable that on the Sunday before the Treat there were very special services in the church, made gay with banners and floral decorations. This latter certainly seemed of immemorial tradition at All Saints' up to a few years ago.[1] A Sunday School Treat of almost exactly the same type is held at St Mary's to this day, but in recent years All Saints' has changed to the more familiar pattern of a coach trip to a neighbouring seaside town.

The fact that the hymn-sheet mentioned was for the twelfth anniversary in 1836 confirms that the Sunday School was established in 1824, the very year that Lyte arrived in Brixham. Indeed in 1825 the Sunday School teachers gave the church a large silver paten which is still occasionally used. Lyte's daughter,[2] probably referring to Lyte's later years in Brixham, says that there were 700–800 children and 70–80 teachers in the Sunday School; Lyte himself in 1832 had claimed fewer teachers but nearly 1,000 children.[3] Probably the 1,000 students (representing over fifteen per cent of the town's population) included adult or near-adult mariners who were learning to read in the Sailors' Sunday School, and other late teenagers who had long since outgrown the day-school age group. Lyte observed in the above sermon that the majority of Brixham ships were in port on Sundays, which gave a priceless opportunity for Sunday School work. How could nearly 1,000 children crowd into the school-rooms which only held 200 on week-days? Possibly rooms outside the National Schools, or All Saints' Church, were used as well, or the classes may all have been at the schools, but in relays. The 1833 Abstract of Education Returns mentions that the Brixham National Schoolroom was a commodious building, and that 250 children then attended daily and 820 on Sundays.[4]

We must now return to the District Church of Lower Brixham. Very

[1] W. A. Earp, *op. cit.*
[2] *Remains,* p. xxiv.
[3] H. F. Lyte, *Commonplace Book,* p. 500.
[4] Quoted in a letter from the National Society to the author, 10.5.1972.

soon after Lyte's arrival the church had to be enlarged, so great were the
crowds that the new Minister was drawing. The exact date of the enlargement does not survive in parish or diocesan records, but a Committee
Minute of the Incorporated Church Building Society (21 February 1825)
records that the Rev. H. F. Leyte (*sic*) had applied for financial aid
towards enlarging the Church at Lower Brixham. It was resolved that
'in consideration of the special circumstances of the case' a grant of £700
should be made. This was a very large sum for the times, equal to two
thirds of the sum raised to pay for the church in the first place. A condition
was attached that 700 of the additional sittings should be free and un-
appropriated for ever. Lyte tells us that by 1832 the number of seats had
been enlarged from 600 to 1,300, which meant that all the additional seats
were to be free—a great blessing when so many of the people were unable
to pay pew rents. The Archdeacon of Totnes' testimonial to Lyte when the
latter was seeking appointment as Vicar of Crediton in 1835 stated that
All Saints' had been twice enlarged after Lyte's arrival (the second
enlargement being in 1827), and that the church then had sittings for
1,800. We prefer Lyte's own figure of 1,300 as it is quite plainly written
by him in his *Commonplace Book* and fits in with his statement there that
more than half the seats were for the poor.[1] Lyte's grand-daughter Miss
A. M. M. Hogg also gives 1,300 in her letter to Miss E. E. Hunt, 5
December 1925.[2]

The lay-out of the enlarged church is given in a plan, dated 1857, still
kept in the belfry. From this it is clear that the enlargement consisted in
the addition of two transepts, with a corresponding increase in the size
of the galleries. The external appearance of Lyte's enlarged church is well
known from contemporary drawings. Lyte's own estimate of it, 'externally it is clumsy but it is neat and commodious within',[1] was generous;
Walter Maxwell-Lyte has described it, not too unfairly, as 'a hideous
barn-like building'.[3]

Faced with such a rapidly expanding charge, Lyte soon found it
necessary to have a curate, whose stipend he had to provide out of his own
pocket. His first assistant was the Rev. J. Harrington, who held office
from September 1826 until January 1828. His successor, the Rev. J. B.
Goodwin, was at Brixham from June 1829 until his death, at the early
age of twenty-six, in August 1832. Various other curates followed,

[1] H. F. Lyte, *loc. cit.*
[2] Lyte family papers.
[3] *British Weekly*, 3.4.1947.

notably John Roughton Hogg, a graduate of Christ's College, Cambridge who came in July 1835 and remained until Lyte's death, marrying the latter's daughter and succeeding him as Incumbent.

One difficulty Lyte had to face was the fact of his wife being a Methodist. Her father, though always an Anglican, was friendly with the Methodist leaders. Lyte's biography states that Dr Maxwell entertained John Wesley at Falkland when he came that way to preach; he was also 'intimately acquainted' with Lady Huntingdon and he used to praise Whitefield greatly. At the time of the Evangelical Revival, Methodists and Evangelical Anglicans had, of course, a very great deal in common. With this background, and being herself greatly impressed by the Methodist preachers, Mrs Lyte joined a Methodist society. According to Garland, page 25, this greatly surprised her father and at the time was much resented by her stepmother. The standing of Nonconformists in the early nineteenth century being much lower than it is to-day, this was a far-reaching step for a woman of Anne Lyte's position to take.

Lyte himself always accepted this position with the utmost tolerance and sympathy, and never complained about it in any letters that survive. Several writers have made much of the fact that when Lyte and his wife drove off to Sunday morning service each week in their little pony-chaise, 'Lyte would descend from the carriage and with charming old-world courtesy he would give his arm to his lady and lead her up the steps of the chapel and then proceed to his own church, calling for her on the way home.'[1] In return Mrs Lyte would attend the Sunday evening service at All Saints', although the more influential members of the congregation would not have been present at that hour.

In fact this situation probably caused Lyte much more difficulty than popular accounts have suggested. Drury, for example, has said:[2]

'One cannot, however, help thinking that the religious unsettle-ment, which later manifested itself in part of Lyte's congregation and caused the last days of his life to be shadowed with not a little grief and anxiety may have been in part at least due to Mrs Lyte's insensitiveness to the loyalty and sympathy due to her husband's position. His gentle consideration for her predilections was certainly greater than her regard for his repute.'

This refers to the later defection of some of Lyte's congregation to the Plymouth Brethren and other Nonconformist denominations.

[1] W. Maxwell-Lyte, *British Weekly*, 3.4.1947.
[2] T. W. E. Drury, *Henry Francis Lyte—A Memorial Discourse* (Lecture published by Dublin University Press, 1948).

Drury's remarks are borne out in a letter from Walter Maxwell-Lyte to the then Headmaster of Portora, 8 March 1948,[1] which mentions that Mrs Lyte 'kept up an intensely religious correspondence on extreme "Salvation Army" lines with her Wesleyan cronies'. We have only been able to trace one letter of this kind, a copy of which was given to Walter Maxwell-Lyte in 1947 by the Rev. G. Stuart Cann, then Methodist Superintendent at Leamington Spa, who had been born at a house next door to Berry Head. The letter, written by Mrs Lyte to Marianne Drake, one of her former housemaids, on 10 July 1829 contains such language as:

> 'I humbly trust that you will go on as you have begun, depending on the grace and mercy of God in Jesus Christ to keep you in the path of duty. Many have commenced their journey through life well, but from some temptation have fallen away and returned to the principles and practices of an evil world. Remember, Marianne, that nothing less than the power and love of God can preserve you amidst the numberless dangers that surround you . . . Your sincere friend, Anne Lyte'.

Mr Cann mentions in his correspondence that in another letter Mrs Lyte expressed her joy that Marianne had joined the Wesleyans. When she later returned to Brixham she joined the same class as Mrs Lyte; Mr Cann knew Marianne personally when he was a boy.

Be this as it may, Lyte remained completely loyal and affectionate to his wife to the end, and there is no indication at all that he was put out by his wife's Methodist affiliation.

While on family affairs, we should add that over these early years in Brixham Mrs Lyte gave birth to two more sons. John Walker Maxwell Lyte—his second name commemorating the Rev. George Walker of the Siege of Londonderry—was born at Burton House on 2 January 1825 and baptised by his father on 14 July. The baptism was almost certainly at the District Church, indeed the local tradition is that he was the first to be baptised in the All Saints' font. The baptism was however entered at St Mary's, the former not yet being a parish church. Farnham Maxwell Lyte was born at Burton House on 10 January 1828 and baptised by his father at the District Church on 19 June. This completed the family of three sons and one (surviving) daughter. The correspondence shows them to have been a united family all their lives; this is perhaps as convenient place as any to summarise their history.

[1] Portora papers.

The eldest son Henry went to Christ Church, Oxford from 1836–39 but left without obtaining a degree. He was evidently self-indulgent and lacking in scholarly discipline, as Mrs Lyte mentions in a letter to her husband on 23 July 1838 when Lyte was staying at Geneva with Henry and Anna Maria. He made a runaway marriage with Emily Prettyjohn, the pretty daughter of a local tollkeeper, at Copenhagen on 10 June 1843.[1] The family soon forgave him for this. In September 1833, when almost fifteen, he had a serious accident through 'playing incautiously with fire works'[2] which caused a large wound covering the whole of his side and the upper part of a thigh. In the early stages his death was expected daily but he somewhat miraculously recovered, despite the limitations of Dr Denmark's rather primitive medical treatment, which involved bathing the wound in copper sulphate solution and other unpromising medicaments. The only clue we have discovered about his later life is in *Alumni Oxonienses*[3] where under Henry's own son John's entry, Henry is said to have been in the Army at St Helier, Jersey (apparently following in his grandfather's footsteps). Henry died at Yarmouth aged thirty-seven on 3 June 1856; his funeral notice in a local paper[4] gives no details of his career.

The second son John was at New College, Oxford from 1843–6 but also left without a degree.[5] However he shared his father's cultural interests and was almost as keen as H. F. Lyte on the library at Berry Head. Among the family papers are some testimonials he obtained in 1847 when seeking a post as a librarian. He married Emily Jeanette Craigie, daughter of Lt.-Col. John Craigie of the Bengal Army, at St George's, Hanover Square on 24 June 1847, his father officiating. Just over a year later, on 28 July 1848, he died of scarlet fever when only twenty-three. By this time, however, his son was born who was to become distinguished as Sir Henry Maxwell-Lyte, Deputy Keeper of Public Records and author of the well-known histories of Eton and of Oxford University.[6]

Farnham, the youngest son, was the most successful of the three. He entered Christ's College, Cambridge in 1846, obtained his BA in 1851 and MA in 1863. He was an Associate of the Society of Civil Engineers and was a pioneer in wet-plate photography, being awarded the Honorary Fellow-

[1] Walter Maxwell-Lyte's notes and his *British Weekly* article, *loc. cit.*
[2] H. F. Lyte, letter to Samuel Wilberforce, 11.11.1833 (Lyte family papers).
[3] Joseph Foster, *Alumni Oxonienses 1715–1886*, Vol. 3 (1888), p. 887.
[4] *Yarmouth Free Press*, 7.6.1856.
[5] Joseph Foster, *loc. cit.*
[6] The hyphenated surname was adopted by Deed Poll by Sir Henry in 1897.

ship of the Royal Photographic Society. In 1851 he married Eleanora
Julia, daughter of Cornelius H. Bolton of Faithlegg, Co. Waterford,
Ireland. Owing to poor health he lived in France from 1853–80; he was
well-known at Baguères in the Pyrenees, where he engaged in meteoro-
logical observations.[1] He died suddenly on 4 March 1906 aged seventy-
eight, his funeral being at St Mary's, The Boltons, Kensington.[2] H. F.
Lyte wrote from Rome to Farnham on 26 November 1846, just as the
latter was starting at Cambridge: 'I trust, too, that you will be diligent
in your attendance on lectures, chapels &c., and let there be one at least
of our family who will pass through College with credit.' John Maxwell-
Lyte, Walter's brother, wrote of Farnham on 19 August (?1947): 'Being
thoroughly unbusinesslike he lost all his fortune over such schemes as
supplying Paris with arms during the Franco-Prussian War.' Farnham
was much admired in Torbay circles in his younger days and he was
elected Master of the Freemasons' lodge at Brixham in 1851 at the
unusually early age of twenty-three.

As to the Lytes' daughter Anna Maria, we shall hear more of her as the
wife of Lyte's curate and successor as incumbent of Lower Brixham
Church, J. R. Hogg. She was evidently educated at home, like her
brothers, for most of her childhood. In 1837 when she was fifteen, however, her parents sent her for about two years to a private school at
Hammersmith called 'The Cedars', whose Headmistress was a Miss Fryer.
A letter from Mrs Lyte to her husband, undated but clearly of this
period, mentioned that Anna Maria was very prone to be led astray:
'If with those who are safe and stirling (sic) characters her mind would
lean towards what is good—But if with such as are the reverse her
disposition affords no obstacles to her going the way of the multitude.'
Possibly this is why Anna Maria was sent to the school; it does seem that
more than one of the Lyte children were handicapped by this weakness
of resolve, which may in part have been inherited from H. F. Lyte's
immediate ancestors. At all events Anna Maria's life worked out happily
for she married the Rev. J. R. Hogg and lived with him and their four
daughters at Berry Head for many years. It seems from Mrs Lyte's
letters that even in 1838 she cherished a hope that Anna Maria might
marry Mr Hogg, who had already been with them three years. Mrs
Lyte had visited Hogg's parents (his father was a Church of England
incumbent) at their home near Kettering, and was immensely impressed
by the Hoggs, as her letters show.

[1] J. A. Venn, *Alumni Cantabrigienses, Part 2, 1752–1900*, 1951, Vol. 4, p. 248.
[2] *The Times*, 6.3.1906.

A few facts about Lyte's social life at this time may be gleaned from his manuscript *Book of Facts, Fancies &c.* commenced on 15 October 1826. There are only a few entries but they include the following:

'*30 October* (1826). Dined at Mr Buller's to-day. Hon[bl] Capt[n] Pellew told many naval stories. Sir Thomas Acland[1] and Lady Acland there, also Mr Newman of Landridge MP for Exeter . . . The Aclands gave me a kind invitation to Killerton.

1 November. Had a long discussion with Sir T. Acland on Catholic Emancipation, which he supported on the grounds of expediency— he takes it for granted that the Catholics must in the end be emancip- ated and we had better do it with as good a grace as possible. Mrs Buller was in great fear lest Sir T. should make a convert of me.

8 November. Dined to-day at Mr Buller's again—Col. Morshead, Mr Hull, Mr G. Newman, &c. of the company.'

Nothing very significant occurs in the further brief entries ending on 20 November—presumably all these dates were in 1826 for the entries appear continuous. After this there appears suddenly an entry dated April 1833: 'It is astonishing how ignorant persons are who possess tolerable information on other subjects on the subject of Religion. I read a few days ago while ill of influenza Bulwer's Eugene Aram. Who cd. believe that the author a member of Parliament imagines that it is the custom of the Protestant Church to pray for the dead, yet so it is in Vol. 3 pages 72 and 73, "The Curate wiped his eyes and prepared to utter, with a quivering but earnest voice, this prayer for the dead" . . . What an admirable legislator must such a Senator as the author make on some of the subjects now discussed in Parliament.' This shows Lyte's Evangelical sympathies at the time.

Mr Buller was in effect Lord of the Manor of Brixham (ownership of the ancient Manor being in fact divided among several), resident at the rebuilt but ancient Lupton House. He was the local MP[2]. and grandson of the High Court judge Sir Francis Buller, Bt., to which title he later succeeded. In 1858 he was created the first Baron Churston. The Bullers had a family aisle or 'pew' in St Mary's, Brixham and Lupton House was still in St Mary's parish after Lower Brixham parish had been carved out of it. But Buller seems to have had a special interest in the new District Church and he had been one of the two Petitioners (the other being the Vicar of Brixham) seeking permission for the original 1816 chapel to be

[1] M.P. for the County of Devon, 1812–18, 1820–31.
[2] Conservative MP for South Devon 1835–58; he assumed the name Yarde- Buller by Royal Licence in 1860.

licensed for public worship. These extracts show how Lyte, despite his orphan background, at once mixed with the leading families of the county on his arrival at Brixham. Much of this was doubtless due to his attractive personality and cultural gifts; his wife's family connections may have helped him.

It is clear, too, that Lyte was keenly interested in politics. His grand-daughter Miss Hogg wrote many years later: 'He was a very keen politician, and both wrote and worked for the Tory cause.'[1] Francis Gribble wrote[2]: 'Lyte was a Tory with the hatred of Radicals which it was considered proper for the parsons of those days to have, and a great friend of the Radical (sic Tory meant) member Sir John Yarde-Buller.' Gribble goes on to relate how Yarde-Buller, hard-pressed by his Radical opponent at a Parliamentary election, appealed for Lyte's support. So Lyte wrote the verse:

> Oh, blue are the heavens above,
>   And blue is the deep rolling sea
> And blue melting eyes are the eyes we love
>   Yes, blue is the colour for me.

This was said to have tipped the scales and won the seat for the Tories. The *Exeter Flying Post* records how later, on 21 October 1830, Lyte was the chief speaker at a 'true-Blue' dinner at the Clarence Hotel, Exeter with the object of forming a Devon Constitutional Society. Part of the report was as follows:

'He (Mr L) was not one of those who thought the Constitution both in Church and State stood in need of no reparation, for what human work had there yet appeared that could be said to have attained perfection, but knowing how much a building was en-dangered by the removal of a brick or stone by an unskilful architect, he must protest against any innovations on its integrity by unskilful hands—by those who came to it like blind Samsons, ready to pull the fabric about our ears, and crush all in one common ruin—(Hear and Loud Cheers) . . . With regard to taxes which formed such a prominent subject of complaint, he could never dismiss it from his mind, that whatever their amount, they were only the price to be paid for preserving to us national blessings, if not national existence—(Hear, hear)—That it was by means of these sacrifices that England is what she is—that she upheld the weak, and succoured those who

---

[1] Letter to Miss E. E. Hunt, 5.12.1925, Lyte family papers.
[2] F. Gribble, *The Romance of the Men of Devon*, 1912, p. 68.

but for her must have sunk under the strong arm of despotism; that by these means it was that her navies rode triumphant on the ocean, and her Armies carried victory into every part of Europe— (Loud cheering)—These it was that enabled her to stand forward in aid of suffering humanity, and to cause others to say of her that on the favoured head of England the sun never ceased to shine.'[1]

The reader may think that Lyte painted a somewhat rosy picture of England during one of the blacker phases of the Industrial Revolution, but many others of his day seemed likewise blind to the facts.

[1] *Exeter Flying Post*, 27.10.1830.

8

LYTE'S GENEVA JOURNEY—AND OTHER EVENTS OF THE LATE EIGHTEEN-TWENTIES

ONE OF Lyte's most fascinating relics is the leather-bound diary describing his journey to Geneva and back between 28 May and 2 July 1827. This diary had somehow come into the possession of the Wilberforce family and was given to Walter Maxwell-Lyte in December 1947 by Miss Susan Wilberforce of Graffham, Sussex, a grand-daughter of Bishop Samuel Wilberforce, who discovered it in an old desk at her home.

The journey began on 28 May when Lyte boarded the steam-packet at Dartmouth at 6 p.m. His wife stayed at home with the children as often on such occasions, but one or two friends travelled with him, including a Mr de Courtenay and a Miss Perkins. After a rough sea passage which troubled him greatly Lyte arrived at Portsmouth at 10 a.m. on 29 May. The party breakfasted at the Fountain Inn, 'I laying in about 2 lbs of mutton chop to make up for the deficiencies of the past day and night.' From there they took a chaise to Chichester, arriving at 3 p.m., and proceeded by pony phaeton to nearby Lavington Hall. This was the home of the Sargent family whose daughter Emily was to marry Lyte's friend Samuel Wilberforce the following year. Wilberforce does not seem to have been at Lavington when they arrived; Lyte joined him at Paris later on.

The Rev. John Sargent and his wife took Lyte and his friends around the magnificent grounds of Lavington and the next day they went to Graffham Rectory a mile away. Sargent was Rector of Graffham but the Rectory was let to Mrs Smith, a relative of Mrs Sargent, and her niece Mrs Carey. 'I found that Mrs Carey was the widow of dear General Carey from whom I first received the light of the Gospel', Lyte added. Walter Maxwell-Lyte traced the career of Major-General Carey but, like ourselves, was unable to trace how and when Lyte met him. He did, however, serve in Ireland for a few months in 1800 when a Major in the Brigade of Guards.[1]

On 31 May Lyte caught the London coach and arrived in town the same day at 8 p.m. 'I read my portions and thought of my dear friends at

[1] *The Royal Military Calendar,* 3rd edition, 1820, Vol. III, p. 372.

Brixham', he comments characteristically. He stayed in London visiting friends until 5 June. The friends included his wife's kinsmen Lord and Lady Farnham, who received him most hospitably. 'They wanted me to stay with them instead of going abroad and promised to nurse me to my heart's content'—Lyte had evidently had another bout of illness. He also saw Lord Rolle and Sir Thomas Acland on 1 June; on 4 June he met 'a large party' at Lord Farnham's and sat between the Earl of Roden and Lord Mandeville.

On 5 June he left London early by coach for Brighton. Finding he had two days to wait for a ship to France he arranged accommodation and walked down to the Chain Pier. 'How ridiculous the affectation of the Methodists who have got a Greek inscription over one of their chapels—they are an aspiring race and the fashion with them is to be thought learned', he added laconically. On 6 June he made a day trip to Worthing by coach but was not impressed with the place. He dined that day at five, had 'tea' at nine and went to bed at 11 p.m. His weight was eleven stone ten pounds, showing that he was by no means emaciated at the time. Travelling with de Courtenay, he took the 9 a.m. steamer from the Chain Pier on 7 June, arriving at Dieppe at 7.30 p.m. 'I gave some tracts to the sailors, who seemed a very sad set, and left a few books on board for the passengers.'

At Dieppe he met Lord Arundel, who was very friendly and civil. 'I agreed to take a carriage with him to Paris . . . Lord Arundel was chatty but very sore on the Catholic question. We had a good deal of laughing about his passing me off as his chaplain.' Lyte describes their first meal with relish. 'I resolved to remember all our dinners and soupers for dear Anne who will be interested in them. We began with Vermicelli soup, fine John Dory. Then mutton chops and cutlets with pommes à la Maître d'hôtel. Then a bon-bon with partridges, pigeons and a nice sweetbread, the whole crowned with asparagus, cheeses and salad and washed down with 3 bottles of best Chables and Beaune wines. Cost 5 fr. each including wine.' Lyte was evidently something of a gourmet and describes a good many such meals in the diary.

On 8 June they arrived in Paris where Lyte stayed until 12 June, having a turn of illness which Samuel Wilberforce describes in a letter written to Lyte after the journey as 'fainting fits'. It seems that Lyte met Wilberforce in Paris on 9 June and that the two travelled together as far as Geneva. According to Wilberforce's biographer,[1] it had been pre-

[1] A. R. Ashwell, *Life of the Rt Rev. Samuel Wilberforce, DD*, 1879, Vol. 1, pp. 36–7.

arranged that Lyte should go abroad in June 1827 with Wilberforce and
Mr Anderson (later Sir Charles Anderson, a fellow-student with
Wilberforce at Oriel). Wilberforce was a commoner of Oriel at the time
Keble, Pusey and Newman were Fellows of the college.[1] It was planned
that the tour should last until November, but according to Ashwell,
Lyte 'was soon obliged to return home through illness', leaving the
other two to continue their journey. Samuel Wilberforce, destined to be
Bishop of Oxford and of Winchester, was the third son of the famous
William. Twelve years Lyte's junior, he was only twenty-two at this
time and not yet ordained. We have not discovered how their friendship
began but they had a common interest in poetry and much of their
correspondence was on this topic.

On 9 June in Paris the diary records: 'I went however up to
Wilberforce's room and found him as glad to see me as I was to see him'.
On 10 June: 'After service I had to retire to bed and stayed there till
evening when my friends came. Dear Wilberforce most kindly read for
me for an hour or two. There is a benevolence of character about him but
rarely met with.' On 12 June, still in Paris: 'I had some delightful talk
with dear Sam[l] Wilberforce about friends far away. We read a few
stanzas of Lord Byron together.' Lyte and Wilberforce continued together
until 19 June, when they went their different ways. Lyte does not mention
in the diary that his illness was the reason for their separation.

On 12 June they left Paris by diligence on the long journey to Geneva.
Passing through Dijon and Poligny, Lyte awoke on 15 June in the midst
of the Jura hills: 'On arriving at the summit I could not believe my eyes.
The Alps stood before me in all their grandeur, and at their feet was
spread the beautiful and placid Lake Léman in full contrast to their
turbulent majesty—never saw I anything like this. Never can I forget it.'
The same day they reached Geneva, where Lyte stayed until 20 June. On
Sunday, 17 June he attended service in the Chapel of a Hospital and was
much impressed by the sermon, given by a Mr Graham. 'After church I
got my letters and devoured them with avidity . . . We were too late to
go to Mr Malan's service which I deeply regretted as I had promised
myself much in hearing him.'

The next day, however, Lyte and Wilberforce called on Malan, who
was a fashionable Calvinist preacher. 'We afterwards entered into a
conversation on his (Malan's) favourite topic of the full assurance of

[1] *ibid.*, p. 26. Keble resigned his Fellowship and Pusey was appointed Fellow, in
1823, the year in which Wilberforce went up to Oriel.

faith. His view of the subject seems to be this that everyone who believed Jesus to have been the Son of God may be regarded as in a state of salvation. He accordingly addresses all as such and calls on them to live up to their privileges. . . In many respects I am disposed to think Mr Malan right. On some, however, I have my doubts and must continue to think it dangerous to soothe before there is distress. They that are sick need the physician.' Wilberforce was also somewhat worried about Malan's doctrine and discussed it with Lyte in a letter he wrote to him on 11 August 1827[1] after the latter had returned home.

The next day, 19 June, Lyte sought out the librarian, Mr Diodati.

'He seems to be a pleasant, well-informed man but more of a belles lettres man than a classic—I addressed him in Latin and afterwards in Greek but he did not seem to know much of either. After breakfast we went to the library together. Mr Diodati showed me first in the library various printed letters of Calvin and the other reformers. There were two or three of Cranmer's among them but not the desired ones. He next gave me the MSS. which I searched for about five hours but could not find a single one of Cranmer's on any subject. There were, however, many very interesting letters in the different volumes relating to the great men of England. A short one is there of Coverdale's in vol. 109. There is another v. interesting letter from the English Exiles under Mary from Francfort vindicating to Calvin themselves and their creed. There are also two striking ones from Calvin to the King of England and various others of the most interesting nature. I am convinced that there lies in the Geneva library a rich mine of matter relative to the reformers and their times well worth exploring.'

Lyte took the steam-packet for Vevey on 20 June and arrived in Berne by voiture the following evening. On 22 June he intended to make just a day trip to Thun and back, but at Thun he was persuaded to extend his tour. He arranged for his luggage to be sent on from Berne to Basel and that evening he saw the magnificent Jungfrau scenery as previously mentioned. He passed on to Grindelwald and thence to the Oberland where he tramped the snow for three hours, and rode on mules for part of the time: 'Incomparable scenery—never saw anything like it before. Visited the fall of Reichenbach, certainly the finest thing I have yet seen in Switzerland. It descends from height to height for nearly half a mile

[1] Ashwell, *op. cit.,* p. 37.

and falls at last through woody steeps into a lovely green valley.' He went on to Lucerne. 'I remarked that in the Catholic cantons the churches were better than in the others but the people poorer and apparently demoralised. Louis said they hated the Protestants and the parties were in continuous strife.'

On Sunday, 24 June he rose at 3 a.m. and prayed for those dear to him in England: 'My wife, my dear children and all the household. My school, poor L.S. Mr & Mrs H. and all at Brixham. Ah what wd. I not give to be with them at this moment.' At 7 a.m. he breakfasted and then took his place in the voiture. 'It is many years since I travelled before on a Sunday, however it seemed to be more allowable here in this Popish land where I could gain nothing and my charioteer little by staying at home. I found the whole population at their early prayers and immediately afterwards they were all busy in the fields. The profanation of the Sabbath in these Popish countries is frightful to a Protestant. All the shops were open in the Towns as I passed and nothing marked the Sabbath but a little superiority in dress.'

Later that day Lyte arrived in Basel and stayed overnight. The next morning he left by diligence at 11 a.m. and continued his journey via Heidleburg (sic) and took supper at Freybourg. The next morning he was at Kehl: 'a miserable place . . . Many soldiers were around. I cannot say how I was annoyed by the military despotism appearing on every side.' At Carlsruhe Lyte had a full view of the Grand Duke passing in his carriage. 'He is a hard featured ill-looking military man.' Lyte then went on to Heidelberg where he spent the night. Continuing the next day via Mannheim he arrived at Mainz at 4 p.m.; here he put up at an hotel and bought a piece of cloth for his wife. He saw the Cathedral: 'a paltry place full of statues of deposed Electors in their robes and mitres. The whole place is thronged with military.'

The next day Lyte took the steam-boat for Cologne. The scenery was dull but later improved. 'I found I was in the land of tobacco—literally every man had his long elastic hooka in his mouth . . . One man drew forth a pipe a full foot longer than any other and came round puffing most furiously. I could no longer stand it but laughed outright. The military Prussians have got possession of this country since the late war.'

Lyte then got into trouble with the Customs. 'I not knowing it was necessary to mention a thing purchased a few miles off and I believe of Saxon or Prussian manufacture omitted to declare my new cloth, in consequence of which I lost it and was obliged to pay about ten shillings to pass some other articles. They were not surly but very determined and would not accept money which I offered them hoping to propitiate them.'

He saw the sights of Cologne and spent the night there, but he was up at 3 a.m. not being able to sleep. He took the coach to Aix-la-Chapelle, and saw the fine old Gothic Town Hall which was once the residence of Charlemagne, whose tomb was in the Cathedral. In the Cathedral Lyte had an interesting talk with a Protestant from Liège. Lyte said to him: 'Bien des chandelles, très peu de lumière'—*he* said if they were not conscious of darkness they would not have so many candles! The gentle-man 'mentioned many examples of Catholic bigotry and intolerance' and hoped that the English would not grant the Papists emancipation.

At 8 a.m. he arrived at Brussels, read his portions and walked around the town. At 1 p.m. he left for Ghent where he went to hear the nuns chant their vespers. 'There were 1,600 of them in the Chapel and their appearance with the linen envelope on their heads was very striking. The singing was sweet and the organ especially so.'

At 6 a.m. on Sunday, 1 July Lyte arrived at Ostend. Here he was fascinated by the Annual Procession in honour of St Peter and described it in great detail, from the old priest under a canopy surrounded by little girls dressed in sky blue with wings on their backs and bows and arrows in their hands, to the Virgin in full dress with the infant Saviour in her arms, borne by a band of four. The procession went around to various altars in a service of singing and elevating the Host at each of them. At the end the sea was blessed and multitudes sprang in to bathe.

The next day Lyte was up at 2.30 a.m. and at 4 a.m. sailed for England by steam-boat. 'We lost sight of the Continent at about 7 o'clock and saw the English shore about ten, with what pleasure I shall not say.' Here the diary ends. Having outlined the chronological sequence of events, however, we now take a second look at the diary inasfar as it gives considerable insights into Lyte's habits and character.

He was a very devout man. Typically on this holiday he rose at 6 a.m. and read and prayed for two hours or more each day, usually before breakfast. His daily Scripture readings over this period included a passage from the Psalms and a portion of I or II Samuel. He loved distributing tracts (some being in French) to any likely people he met. He was very much an Evangelical, yet he was peculiarly attracted by Roman Catholic priests and ceremonies and always commented on them in great detail. He was very anxious that the true Gospel, as he understood it, should be preached in the churches. Wherever possible on the journey he attended church, and he always gave a keen assessment of the sermon. At Ostend (1 July) for example, he says of a service in the English Church: 'We had the service respectably performed, but nothing like the Gospel.'

The diary also brings out Lyte's wide cultural interests. He could speak Greek, Latin and French, but not difficult subjects in the latter tongue. He spoke no German. He loved visiting the libraries at the various towns through which he passed, and enjoyed discussing literature with anyone. He was fairly knowledgeable in the world of science and knew the names of many wild flowers. At Paris he greatly admired Cuvier's preparations of skeletons: 'I remained in this forest of bones for an hour. Then went to the fossils and minerals' (11 June). At Tomurre on 13 June Lyte found a quarry full of fossil shells, some of which he took for his son Henry. Sometimes there is a little pseudo-science, for example at Thun on 22 June: 'The river at Thun was "as blue as the ocean wave". This property of the Swiss water is remarkable and must I think be occasioned by the melting ice, which is blue as it stands in the Glaciers.' In an age when scientific knowledge was still primitive, however, this was excusable.

Lyte always showed a great love for his family and friends in the notes he made in the diary. He missed his family immensely, even on a short absence like this. He longed for letters and was tremendously sorry for those who were sick—he was plainly a man of intense emotions. Some-times he seemed rather condescending towards the poor; on 12 June, for example, he said he was glad to be riding in the coupé of the diligence, as the other parts were 'crammed with filthy women and children.' On 29 May at Portsmouth he wrote: 'We saw some hideous scenes of sensual brutality—women running about after sailors and they staggering about drunk in the open daylight. I cannot say how I was shocked.' But we must not make the mistake of judging Lyte in 1827 by the criteria of unshockable modern society!

Lyte was still attractive to the opposite sex. Thus on 24 June he wrote: 'We stopped for two hours at mid-day near the fortress Aarburg. I went out in the fields and presently was joined by a young and handsome Bernoise who I believe was no better than she should be. She made several advances to me but I repelled her by giving her two tracts and a lecture which appeared to abash her. Poor girl I may have misunderstood her, but what I said could not wound and might benefit her.'

The diary shows that Lyte suffered severe pain and illness, even at this stage when he appeared generally to be at the height of his powers. On 7 June he wrote: 'I suffered excessively from jolting—I had a severe pain

through my chest and right shoulder blade.' The next day, arriving at
Paris at 8 p.m. he wrote: 'I suffered a good deal in the night from a
violent pain in the shoulder blade passing through my chest.' On 9 June
he added: 'However I was in great pain and hardly able to sit up. No
letters for me at the Post Office and ill in body and dejected in mind I cd.
hardly work my way back to the hotel . . .' (later that day), 'I returned
home and lay down very unwell. Dr Mc.Loughlin called. He is a mere
ass and knows as much about medicine as his grandmother. However
I let him prescribe and took my own medicines.' 10 June: 'In seeing the
Dr this morning I believe that in my hurry I gave him a franc instead of
a napoleon—either was more than he deserved. Felt better.' It seems very
likely that even now Lyte was suffering from tuberculosis, in which case
it was a near miracle that he survived twenty years more of his very
arduous parish work.

After this journey a regular correspondence went on between Lyte and
Samuel Wilberforce; some fifteen letters from Samuel have been
preserved in the Lyte family papers. Wilberforce seems to have been very
attached to Lyte. He did not accept the latter's offer of a first curacy at
Lower Brixham, on the grounds that he wished to be fairly close to
Lavington (he was in fact ordained to a title at Checkendon, near Henley-
on-Thames). Wilberforce was very anxious, however, that Lyte should
officiate at his wedding. Lyte was always very slow in replying to
Wilberforce's letters, pleading as an excuse the pressure of his parish work.
It was for this reason alone, as far as can be seen from the correspondence,
that Charles Simeon and not Lyte conducted the wedding at Lavington
Church on 11 June 1828.

Wilberforce was also very pressing that Lyte should stay with him and
meet his famous father. This offer Lyte was again very slow to take up,
although he did eventually meet William Wilberforce. Samuel actually
played a joke on Lyte in his letter to him of 24 September 1833, when he
wrote 'Did you write *The Notebook of a Country Clergyman* recently
published? If not tell me what you think of it. If you did let me know and
I will give you my candid opinion'. But Samuel had of course written
the book himself! Even in his next letter to Lyte he kept up the pretence,
asking 'Has my critical eye rightly detected your able pen in the story of
"Confession"? Do tell me.'[1]

In the first of the two letters quoted Wilberforce announced that his
sister-in-law Caroline Sargent was to marry H. E. Manning, who was

[1] 'Confession' was one of the stories in the *Notebook*.

then Rector of Lavington and later to become a Cardinal. Wilberforce describes Manning thus: 'a pious and pleasant man of superior abilities and well calculated to make her (Caroline) happy.'

According to Ashwell, Lyte stayed with Wilberforce at Brighstone Rectory in the summer of 1835 when Manning and 'Mr T. Acland' were among the other guests.[1] The same author mentions[2] that during his celebrated preaching tour for S.P.G. in Exeter Diocese in the autumn of 1839 Samuel Wilberforce visited Brixham and Dartington. In this case Lyte's name is not mentioned, but it seems highly probable that Wilberforce preached for him. The last letter from Wilberforce to Lyte which we have found is dated 12 December 1833. It ends: 'Do answer *speedily*—as time is of importance to me. Ever with both our kind[st] remembrances, Believe me to remain, your very aff[te] Samuel Wilberforce.' Who knows how Lyte's friendship with Wilberforce would have grown had the former been a less reluctant correspondent?

We end this chapter by recounting two or three other events which happened about this time. On 21 July 1828 H.R.H. The Duke of Clarence (soon to become William IV) paid an official visit to Brixham as Lord High Admiral. He landed at the harbour, visited the Government works and sailed around the bay in the steam-packet *Lightning*. The Brixham inhabitants presented him with an Address of good-will, together with a piece of the stone on which William of Orange first set foot when he landed in England, at Brixham, in 1688. The chip of the stone was contained in a case of Heart of Oak over 800 years old, from the old Totnes bridge, beautifully lined with velvet.[3] Other accounts say that the Duke was met at the landing stage by Lyte and a surpliced choir, and that later William IV presented Berry Head House to Lyte as a gift.[4] The newspaper accounts, however, make no mention of Lyte and the choir, nor does Charles Gregory in his classic guide to Brixham.[5] Walter Maxwell-Lyte's notes say that Lyte made the presentation to the Duke, and it is possible that he did, but the matter must be regarded as uncertain. Lyte definitely did not receive Berry Head as a gift,[6] and we doubt whether he would

[1] A. R. Ashwell, *op. cit.,* Vol. I, p. 85.
[2] *ibid.,* p. 147.
[3] *Exeter Flying Post,* 24.7.1828; *Western Luminary* (Exeter), 29.7.1828.
[4] e.g. F. A. Jones, *Famous Hymns and their Authors,* 3rd edition, 1905, p. 12.
[5] *Brixham in Devonia,* 1896, pp. 58–9.
[6] See below, p. 90.

have had a surpliced choir as early as 1828, at which time he was still an Evangelical.[1]

It must have been about 1828 or 1829, too, when Lyte carried out his biggest scientific investigation—the excavation of Ash Hole Cavern, which was a short distance from Berry Head, on the harbour side. Two detailed accounts of this are given in Lyte's *Commonplace Book*,[2] the earlier one being a copy of a letter to the Rev. John Mc.Enery which he wrote on 12 November 1829. Mc.Enery, who was for many years Chaplain at Tor Abbey, Torquay, was the first person to explore Kent's Cavern, a stalactite cave on the edge of that town, and he had himself made a slight excavation of Ash Hole Cavern, finding a small piece of Roman pottery. Lyte had a seventy-foot shaft dug in one chamber and a twenty-five-foot shaft in another, and found quantities of charcoal, ash and half-consumed human bones, proving that it was a burial cave. He also found pieces of coarse, unglazed Roman pottery, several human skeletons, bits of brass and ivory and animal bones and teeth. Mr Bartlett, a native of Brixham, assisted Lyte in the excavation.[3] While by modern standards Lyte's account has an amateurish ring about it—indeed he confessed to Mc.Enery that he was by no means an expert in the study of bones—it was nonetheless a very creditable undertaking for a busy parish priest in those days.

The last matter we shall mention here is Lyte's part in the Campaign against Catholic Emancipation. Partly because of trouble with Roman Catholics in Ireland and partly because of the new spirit of tolerance growing in Britain, successive Acts of Parliament were passed to ease the lot of Roman Catholics both in England and Ireland. In 1778 an Act was passed allowing Catholics to hold landed property, on taking an oath which did not require them to deny their faith. In 1791 Roman Catholic worship and Catholic Schools became tolerated, and in 1793 Catholics in Ireland were admitted to the franchise, the Universities and the professions. Even after this, however, Catholics in England were still debarred from Parliament, the Universities and a great many public offices. Pressure was mounting for these remaining disabilities to be removed and it seemed that further legislation was imminent. Yet fear of the Roman Church, due partly to buried memories of religious conflict

[1] G. W. D. Addleshaw and F. Etchells, *The Architectural Setting of Anglican Worship*, 1948, p. 213. Leeds Parish Church, completed in 1841, was the first church of any note to have a surpliced choir.

[2] pp. 51, 500f. See also the author's MA Thesis, pp. 130f.

[3] W. Pengelly, *Transactions of the Devonshire Association*, 1870, Vol. IV, p. 75.

in past centuries and partly to the belief that the Catholics would deny freedom of worship to the Protestants if once they regained the upper hand, was still great. Movements arose up and down the country to protest against the possibility of further relief for the Catholics, and Lyte was an ardent supporter of the Protestant cause. He spoke at various 'Protestant Meetings' held in Devon towns in 1828–9, the first of which was at Newton Abbot on 5 November 1828. A good account of this has been given by a local historian[1]; more details of the speeches are given in a local paper.[2]

Colonel Drake of Ipplepen was Chairman of the Newton Abbot meeting and urged the crowd, 'which was the greatest, perhaps, ever seen in Newton'[3], to behave with impartiality and moderation. Hustings had been erected in the street and Union Jacks displayed, in a manner recalling the recent Orange demonstrations in Northern Ireland. The chief speakers were Mr Yarde-Buller, Mr Henry Studdy of Watton Court, near Brixham, and H. F. Lyte. The first two officially moved the acceptance of a Petition to both Houses of Parliament, to be signed by the people of Newton Abbot and its vicinity. The Petition expressed 'strong attachment to the protestant principles by which our civil and religious liberties have hitherto been preserved' and begged Parliament to ensure that 'the protestant constitution of the united kingdom may be preserved entire and inviolate'.

The Rev. J. P. Jones of North Bovey, an Anglican priest of far more tolerant and liberal views than Lyte, moved an amendment asking that the penal code against the Catholics be removed, as the only means of restoring tranquillity to Ireland. It was after this that Lyte spoke 'at great length'. 'We wish to see the Catholics emancipated', he said 'but it is not the sort of emancipation that the Rev. Gentleman (Jones) wishes; we want to see them emancipated from the priests, and from the power of the factious and turbulent demagogues of Ireland. We want to see the manacles struck off their minds—to see them released from the degrading fetters of error and superstition—allowed to think for themselves—endowed with liberty of conscience, free of the bible (*sic*), for he is a freeman only whom the truth makes free and all besides are slaves. (Cheers). One would suppose from the Rev. Gentleman who has spoken before me that there is but a trifling difference between the Protestant and

[1] D. M. Stirling, *History of Newton Abbot and Newton Bushel*, 1830, pp. 55f.
[2] *Western Luminary*, 11.11.1828.
[3] *Devonshire Chronicle and Exeter News*, 20.12.1828.

Roman Catholic Churches . . . it is notorious that the differences between the two churches are most essential . . . Ridley, Latimer, Hooper and Cranmer went to the stake for these differences, yet the Rev. Gentleman says they are not essential . . . the bible proves the Roman Catholic Church to be unscriptural—persecuting—prone to intolerance . . . I fear this Church is exactly the same in spirit as when the fires of Smithfield were lighted up.' The speech was greeted with 'immense and continued cheering'. Mr Jones vainly protested that Lyte was being unfair; his amendment was defeated and the original motion accepted by a huge majority. Thousands more signatures were added to the Petition on 28 November when a great Protestant Dinner was held in the same place; church bells were rung and even salutes of small artillery fired!

Lyte spoke at similar meetings at Totnes on 18 December (for clergy only, with Archdeacon Froude in the chair),[1] at Brixham on 17 February 1829 (at the Market House with Mr Yarde-Buller in the chair),[2] and at the Old London Inn, Exeter on 28 February.[3] At all these meetings Lyte had a heavy majority in his favour, though we note that at a meeting at Sidmouth at which Lyte was not present the voting was unanimously in favour of the Catholics.[4] At the Exeter meeting Lyte said of the prospects of Emancipation: 'His Majesty had been taken by storm by the Military Commander in Chief (Wellington) and his subalterns.' The newspaper, which was not sympathetic to the Protestants, added of Lyte: 'The rev. gentleman used several violent expressions which we do not think it proper to report.'!

An interesting sequel to the Newton Abbot meeting was an attack on Lyte, who was not named but referred to as a clergyman of the Church of England, in the House of Lords on 23 February 1829 when Lord Rolle rose to present 'a petition from the inhabitants of the county of Devon, against granting further concessions to the Roman Catholics.'[5] Lord King responded: 'The noble lord has stated that this petition (was) passed at one of the most numerous meetings he ever witnessed. Might not the noble lord have added, that it was also one of the most disorderly?' On Lord Rolle's reply that the meeting was 'constitutionally conducted', Lord King countered: 'Then perhaps the noble lord thinks that it was proper and decorous for a clergyman of the church of England to act as a

[1] *Devonshire Chronicle and Exeter News*, 20.12.1828.
[2] *ibid*. 21.2.1829.
[3] *ibid.*, 28.2.1829.
[4] *ibid.*, 3.1.1829.
[5] *House of Lords Debates,* 1829, cols. 467–8.

fugleman on the occasion, and to direct, by signs, who should be heard, and who should not.' Lord Rolle then claimed that while the supporters of the petition had no fugleman, a fugleman did act for the Roman Catholics and appeared in a very conspicuous situation.

The Bishop of Exeter (William Carey) then rose to defend Lyte. He understood that it was not the case that the clergyman had acted indecorously. 'So far from putting himself forward on the occasion, (he) did not make his appearance until towards the end of the meeting, for the purpose of delivering his sentiments on the question. It was a question in which the interests of the church were particularly involved; and he could not see why a clergyman should be debarred from giving his opinion on a proposition which affected the constitution of the country.'

W. Maxwell-Lyte quotes from Lyte's speech at the Exeter meeting[1] as follows: 'I have heard since I entered this room of new honours likewise. I have, I understand, been shown up doubtless by the kind assistance of friends here, in the House of Peers as the very impersonification of bigotry, the leader and fugleman of this late County meeting . . . Truly I would not as a clergyman desire a higher distinction than to be attacked by Lord King and vindicated by my Diocesan.' This was not reported by the newspaper, possibly being regarded as one of the violent expressions unsuitable for publication! To describe Lyte's words as violent was perhaps to overstate the case, but even so a close study of the text of these Protestant speeches of Lyte's gives the impression that he could be a bigot when carried away by his powerful emotions.

Despite Lyte's fervour, this cause was lost. The prospects of a rebellion of the Irish Catholics and the security risk of tying up a large part of the Army in Ireland convinced the Government that they would have to yield. The objections of George IV, a bitter anti-Catholic, were overcome; the Emancipation Bill passed the Commons by 320 votes to 142 on 5 March 1829. It was subsequently passed by the Lords and received the Royal Assent on 13 April. Henceforth Catholics were admitted to the franchise and Catholic Peers and MPs were allowed to sit and vote in their respective Houses.

[1] Walter Maxwell-Lyte seems to have had a copy of this speech, which we have not been able to find.

9

LYTE IN THE EIGHTEEN-THIRTIES

THE FIRST item of note in the new decade was Lyte's Anti-Slavery Campaign in Brixham, which took place late in 1830. Various short accounts of Lyte's life[1] say that he co-operated with William Wilberforce for the abolition of the slave trade. This is perhaps a slight overstatement in that Lyte was too young to have been a real contemporary of William Wilberforce, who died in 1833. His bill rendering the slave trade illegal was passed as early as 1807 when Lyte was but a lad of fourteen. In his letter to Samuel Wilberforce dated 11 November 1833 Lyte congratulates himself on having conversed with William Wilberforce the previous summer at Bath, but the letter sounds as if Lyte had scarcely met him before.

None the less Lyte organised a petition to Parliament from the people of Brixham requesting that slavery be finally abolished. Although the 1807 Act had made the slave *trade* illegal, existing slaves had in many cases still been retained. A printed copy of the Petition, subscribed 'Brixham, 15 November 1830', is attached without written comment to page 251 of Lyte's *Commonplace Book*. John Maxwell-Lyte's letter to his brother Walter, dated 19 August (1947?), says that the Petition was preceded by a mass meeting at Brixham on 10 December 1833 but the latter date cannot be right. The printed sheet is headed: 'Copy of Petition to be sent to Parliament from the Inhabitants of Brixham and its vicinity, for the Abolition of Slavery in the British Dominions.' The Petition ran: 'When an end was put by the British Parliament to the Slave Trade it was hoped that on the principles of consistency the downfall of Slavery itself would soon follow. If it be wrong to make men slaves it surely cannot be right to keep them such. But after an interval of twenty-three years this debasing system . . . is still found to exist without any material abatement . . . We entreat you to take immediate and effectual steps for their relief, and to adopt such measures as in your wisdom you shall deem best for the early and entire abolition of Slavery throughout the British Dominions.' Lyte was more successful in this cause than in his

[1] e.g. W. Maxwell-Lyte, *British Weekly*, 3.4.1947.

efforts to block Catholic Emancipation, for in 1833 slavery was totally abolished throughout the British Dominions.

Soon after this Lyte was involved in another Petition, but this one was addressed to himself. It was from the people of Brixham who begged him not to leave them, as it was rumoured he might, to become Perpetual Curate of Penzance. To understand the situation we must go back a few years to 19 September 1825 when H. F. Lyte wrote a letter to his wife from Drogheda; we may guess that he had been visiting his old friend John Kerr, now Incumbent of Termonfeckin some five miles from the former town.[1] The letter is obviously in reply to one from Mrs Lyte expressing dissatisfaction with life at Brixham. Mrs Lyte's letter cannot be found but Garland, pages 25–6, prints a summary of what seems to have been her letter. Garland seems to have got his facts somewhat confused, for he writes as though this letter of Mrs Lyte's came just before the Petition to Lyte in 1831, whereas Prime Minister George Canning, who Mrs Lyte thought might procure her husband a better living, died in 1827. The contents of Mrs Lyte's letter as quoted by Garland strongly suggest that it was in fact written not in 1831 but in 1825, and that Lyte's letter to his wife from Drogheda was the reply to it.

According to Garland, Mrs Lyte expressed in her letter her discontent with the living conditions at Burton House. It was rather dreary and was shut in at the back, like so many Brixham houses, by a sheer rock face only a few feet away. The view from the house was uninteresting. The stipend was only £80 p.a., out of which rent had to be paid. There was a chance of a better living at Penzance which Mrs Lyte thought was more suited to her husband's talents—at any rate this is what Garland says, but we believe it to be an erroneous interpolation. Continuing Garland's version, Lyte replied to this letter that Anne ought to make sure that the change was God's will for them; if so she could write to Canning and ask his support. 'Later', Garland concludes, 'Mrs Lyte learned someone had been appointed to the vacancy, so the incident was closed, his wife feeling it was the will of God that he should remain in Brixham and she continued to cheerfully assist him in his ministry.'

In fact Lyte's letter to his wife runs as follows:

'You are I fear engaged in rather a wildgoose speculation respecting Cornwall and I much fear that in consulting Mr John or any other professional man you will only be going into needless expense without the least prospect of success. Indeed I do not see what Mr John

[1] Rev. G. Browne, letter to W. Maxwell-Lyte, 20.10.1947.

can possibly do in the matter. However, if this or any other proceeding would contribute in the event of its failure to make you more comfortable at Brixham I should be most happy to assent to it. With regard to the livings however which you have mentioned they are I think both disposed of. St Just certainly is and Paul's has been applied for. I think your way of proceeding with regard to this or any other matter should rather be to apply to Mr C. Moundy or his brother the member and to get him to speak to Mr Canning to speak again to Ld. Liverpool or the Chancellor in my behalf. Mr Canning might be reminded of the circumstance of his having heard me at Saltram and be informed that I was wasting if you please to call it so my life and talents on Brixham where I had but £80 a year. This I think shd. be your project. I call it *yours* because I cannot conscientiously in any way join in it. I feel that I am now useful and can take no step to remove myself out of my present sphere. Anything however that you can do I shall regard as providential and I sincerely trust that it may tend to your happiness. For this my dear Anne believe me that I entertain the most tender regard but still I must not set your (shall I call it) caprice above the duty we both owe to God . . . Do what you think best in the matter. If you are successful in obtaining anything it will be for us to consult together respecting my accepting it and if not I hope that you will quietly acquiesce and endeavour to make yourself happy in the place and with the numberless blessings that God has assigned to you and which by a different conduct from that which you have hitherto pursued you might make much more numerous than they now are.'

If there is a very mild element of censure in this letter, it at least shows understanding and a Christian approach towards a wife who wanted to move before her husband had been in Brixham eighteen months and before he had achieved his promised status of an incumbent.

It was nearly six years later, in point of fact, when in 1831 Lyte became a candidate for the living of Penzance. A testimonial letter written to Lyte by the Rev. Thomas Pascoe, Vicar of St Hilary, in 1835 when Lyte was seeking appointment as Vicar of Crediton, gives the key to the situation. Pascoe, who was Lyte's incumbent when he was Lecturer of Marazion, was still in the same parish when in October 1835 he wrote: 'You had our best wishes and those of a great majority of the inhabitants of Penzance when at a subsequent period (i.e. in 1831) you became a candidate for the Perpetual Curacy of that town, a situation for which I

considered you eminently qualified in every respect, and where you had
given such general satisfaction during the time you performed its various
duties in the absence of Mr Le Grier.'

It seems most likely that Lyte was invited to apply for the living of
Penzance on the recommendation of his many friends and admirers, both
at Penzance and at Marazion which was three miles away. News of the
possible move soon spread to Brixham and the Petition was sent begging
him to stay. Amongst the treasures of All Saints', Brixham are a copy of
the Petition, along with Lyte's reply, printed in gold on sky-blue glossy
paper, and also the original manuscript of Lyte's reply, written in his
own hand on a very large sheet of paper. The printed document says
that at a meeting of the people of Brixham, held in the vestry of the
'New Church' on 16 May 1831, and then adjourned to the church because
of the numerous attendance, the text of the Address to Lyte was adopted,
and signed 'in less than two days by upwards of nine hundred persons'.
The Address notes with appreciation 'the inestimable benefits which
(under Him who ordereth all things both in Heaven and Earth) have
resulted from your residence and labours among us during the last few
years', and that 'bound as we are to you by the strongest ties of affection
and regard, in consequence of your numerous acts of kindness towards us,
and your indefatigable exertions for our welfare, spiritual and temporal,
we need scarcely tell you that the possibility of your being removed
from us into Cornwall, has been to us a source of much sorrow and
regret.' The letter expressed the hope that Lyte would still remain
with them, and the document records that a Deputation of Gentlemen
were to wait on Lyte with the Address.

Lyte's reply began as follows:

'Your kind Address to me in the prospect of my removal to
Penzance has gratified and affected, though not surprised me. It is
only in unison with the unvarying kindness which I have experienced
at your hands since I became your Minister. My poor exertions in
that capacity I am sensible that you greatly overrate. It has been my
happiness to have my lot cast in a peculiarly favourable portion of
the Lord's vineyard, and to this circumstance, under God, I am
disposed to ascribe any good that may have been accomplished here.
Your kind acceptance however of my services is not on this account
less entitled to my gratitude, and I can truly say that whatever may
be your kindly feelings towards me they are cordially returned.
My labours here have always been labours of love, and have therefore

been their own reward . . . The state of suspense in which we are at present left is extremely painful both to you and me, and I shall take immediate measures for putting an end to it by requesting the Corporation of Penzance to proceed without further delay to their election.'

In this shrewd reply Lyte made no promise to reject the living if offered it, but he added that in this case: 'be assured, my dear friends, that I will not take any ultimate step without considering what I owe to the people of Brixham'. The evidence already given rather suggests, in fact, that Lyte was not finally offered the living. The reply was composed quickly, for it was dated 18 May 1831.

Before passing on to the next major event we mention one or two other happenings which occurred while the Lytes were at Burton House. H. F. Lyte's elder brother Thomas, as already mentioned, died there in 1831. Thomas' death was soon followed by that of Mrs Lyte's aunt, Philippa Massingberd (aged eighty-three) on 23 July 1831. The much-loved curate J. B. Goodwin died (aged twenty-seven) on 21 August 1832. These three were all buried in Lower Brixham Church, probably under the flagstones, and are the only names in All Saints' Burial Register. A tablet in memory of Goodwin, erected by the Sunday School teachers, was fixed to the church wall and still survives; the others now have no monument.

The Rev. E. Wilcocks succeeded Goodwin and served as curate from April 1833 until March 1835. On 3 November 1831, according to Walter Maxwell-Lyte's notes,[1] Lyte preached a sermon at Holy Trinity, Exeter, which was published by request, but we have not been able to find a copy.

In 1833 the first edition of *Poems, Chiefly Religious* was published, a second edition following in 1841. In his letter to Samuel Wilberforce dated 11 November 1833 Lyte said that this collection of his poems was being published 'really, but not avowedly, for a pet charity.' It was to have been dedicated to Lady Farnham, but she died on 10 October 1833. The book was therefore dedicated to her husband Lord Farnham, the fifth Baron. The foreword takes the form of an open letter to Lord Farnham in which he extols the virtues of Lady Farnham and expresses regret at her passing. It contains fifty-four poems or hymns, nearly all of short length. They include the popular hymn 'When at Thy footstool,

[1] p. 25 of the manuscript notes, as numbered by B. E. N. Lyte.

Lord, I bend' and the New Year hymn 'Hail to another year'.[1] Of these the former is still played on the carillon of chimes at All Saints' Church at 8 a.m. every day, while the latter was for years a favourite at the church, being sung to Lyte's own tune each New Year's day until only a few years ago. There are several metrical Psalms, including Psalm 137, 'How shall we sing the Lord's song in a strange land?', which is the first composition in the book. There are numerous poems on nature and the four seasons, the fine poem 'On a Naval officer buried in the Atlantic' which was afterwards set to music by Sullivan, the touching poem 'On Dreaming of my Mother' and a poem called 'Agnes' which rather suggests that Lyte had in his young days a sad parting from a girl he loved.

This was the only straightforward book of poems published in Lyte's lifetime. After his death, however, his daughter published another substantial collection of his poems as part of the Remains in 1850. In 1868 these two collections were combined in Miscellaneous Poems, of which a second edition appeared in 1875. In 1834 came the first edition of Lyte's greatest work The Spirit of the Psalms, which included from one to five metrical versions of each of the 150 Psalms. This ran to five editions and receives more detailed treatment in Chapter 14.

As a full treatment of Lyte's poems would take more space than is available in a volume of this kind, we must content ourselves by quoting a few of the comments made on Lyte's poems in the literature. The Edinburgh Review in 1834[2] placed Lyte among 'our minor poets, "the twinkling stars", "the miscellaneous o'er", (which) become visible indeed only after the great luminaries of poetry are set . . . Still, many persons . . . feel that the secondary ones have a charm and value peculiarly their own'. This reviewer was pleased to find that 'Religion forms the atmosphere rather than the substance of his poems; and we are happy to find that his alarms, ecclesiastical or civil, have not penetrated into the Muses' bower'. He praises Lyte for 'an evident absence of cant of composition, and of all study for effect'.

Garland, page 19, states that some of Lyte's poems had been likened to those of Keats, and if Lyte had spent his whole time in the study of poetry he would probably have become a famous national poet. Certainly the vast flow of hymns and poems that came from his pen during the three years' enforced rest at Sway and Dittisham, all written when he was

[1] Both Garland and the author of the Remains claim that the New Year hymn was written in December 1846, but this must have been due to confusion with the poem 'January 1st 1847'.
[2] Edinburgh Review, 1834, Vol. 59, pp. 171f.

under twenty-nine and in poor health, invites conjecture as to what his output might have been had not his later days been occupied with such busy pastoral labours and still more illness. On page 29 Garland quotes an earlier edition of the *Encyclopaedia Britannica* as saying of 'The Poet's Plea': 'Its subject and form will rank with one of the poems of Gray.'

T. W. E. Drury, Precentor of St Patrick's Cathedral, Dublin comments in 1948[1]: 'His published poems place him not in the front rank of poets, yet in a deservedly high place. He possessed a lyrical gift, a facility of expression, a sincerity of thought, a gentle spontaneity, a tender sympathy, a love of nature which marked a poet born.' The secret of his success as a hymn-writer, Drury concluded, was that 'allied to his natural poetic gift he had the heart of a genuinely devout Christian. In his hymns there is a singular freedom from the excessive self-abasement and over-emotional language in which the love of God is often couched.'

It was somewhat unusual for a true poet to be involved in such a busy and varied active life which included, as we have seen, militant partisanship in certain political issues. For this reason Lyte's poems, for all their beauty and flights of imagination, have a down-to-earth quality not often seen in other poets. Lyte was indeed a virtual genius. Apart from his poetry he had a flair for almost any kind of study from theology or music to natural science, brilliant wit and oratory, together with a real love of souls and a deep understanding of human beings in whatever state of life.

Early in 1833 an event happened which was profoundly to influence the Lytes' future years. They moved from the dreary Burton House to their delightful and well-known home at Berry Head. This had originally been built from 1806–9 as a military hospital for the Army garrison stationed at Berry Head during the Napoleonic Wars.[2] After the defeat of Bonaparte the troops were withdrawn, and according to Garland, page 26, a Mr Burns opened it as a rest house in 1831. Mrs Lyte had been ill and to help her recuperate the whole family stayed there a fortnight. They were so delighted with it that the Lytes resolved if possible to secure possession of the house, which they did. They were certainly there, with workmen laying out the gardens, on 12 March 1833, when the first of a number of letters from Mrs Lyte to her husband during this period was written. Oppenheim[3] describes the purchase of land by Lyte as follows:

[1] T. W. E. Drury, *Henry Francis Lyte—A Memorial Discourse* (Lecture given 24.5.1948, published by Dublin University Press, 1948).

[2] A. C. Ellis, *Paignton News*, 1.10.1938.

[3] M. Oppenheim, *The Maritime History of Devon*, 1968, p. 95.

'In view of the constant use made of Torbay by the fleets, it was thought advisable to guard the anchorage by batteries, and the 34 George III, cap. 76, settled the purchase of land at Brixham and Berry Head, 120 acres being bought at the latter place. There were built at Berry Head two permanent works and three temporary batteries, mounting altogether 40 guns; after the war the ground and batteries were let on lease, but in 1834 an offer of £1,125 for 21 acres from the Rev. H. T. Lyte (*sic*) was accepted, and the remainder was let subject to three months' notice of resumption for military purposes.'

It is clear from other evidence, however, that Berry Head House and its garden were only rented by the Lytes. The land they bought outright must have been adjacent to the house and was probably the part they called Berry Head Farm. Thus a note by Walter Maxwell-Lyte states that for a long time the Lytes rented the house from the War Office and only after Lyte's death did they purchase it outright. Similarly Ellis (his newspaper article being an extract from the *History of Brixham* which he wrote but did not get published) states[1]: 'Later it (*sc.* Berry Head House) was purchased by his curate and son-in-law, the Rev. J. R. Hogg.' Mrs Lyte actually mentions, too, in a letter soon to be quoted, that they paid a house rent of £10. Doubtless the War Office would have been unwilling to sell the house in 1834 in case it might be needed again for military purposes. Certainly the Lyte and Hogg families later purchased the house and grounds, and Lyte's grand-daughter Miss A. M. M. Hogg lived there until her death in 1933 at eighty-two years of age. In 1936 the house with a small part of the land was sold and became an hotel; the rest of the land was still owned by the Lyte Trustees when purchased by Torbay County Borough in 1969 as an open space.

The house, which remains to-day with moderate alterations as an hotel, is in a magnificent position with the edge of the cliff only a few yards away and commands some of the finest views in Devon. Not only was Mrs Lyte's discontent removed by its charms, but Lyte himself developed a great love for the house, from the grounds of which he could see his red- and brown-sailed trawlers in the harbour and all the beauty of a sunset over Torbay. He employed a number of men to lay out the grounds as a lovely garden and many species of plants were put in. John Maxwell-

---

[1] A. C. Ellis, *loc. cit.*

Lyte was no doubt correct in saying that the Lytes kept 'quite a good table there'.[1]

As regards the Lytes' standard of living at Berry Head we quote a letter Mrs Lyte wrote to her husband on 14 July 1834. Most of Mrs Lyte's letters to her husband mention money in one way or another. She was obviously a good manager of financial affairs, but her letters show that she invariably allowed her husband to make the final decision in matters of finance or business. Even so, she was rather over-anxious about finance and always made her points firmly. The letter runs:

'I have sat up by night and day and made several minute calculations as to our expenditure and I now freely propose to you to keep the house (house rent £10) in all Groceries, Draperies, Meats and Poultry, Carpenters-jobs, Druggists Bills, Coals, candles and soap, Post office Bills, Tin-man's Bills, Masons, Glaziers Bill, Blacksmiths, Servants and Labourers Wages, Expenses and rent of fields, Land tax and poor rates, Cows keeping and three horses and cart (but no carriage)—Doctors Bills, Washing &c., indeed all and every thing that pertains to our present establishment with 4 pupils *for £1,000* per ann., to be paid to me quarterly. Every pupil above 4 you must allow me £15 for in addition—Wine, the Curates Stipend; and Miss Bisset's (governess) salary you must defray; and all Books and carriage for the same—and then with the overplus you can I think begin to pay up arrears; and the interest for borrowed money . . . The Garden I will keep in order for the sum named . . . I think this will give you much leisure, what you are ever desiring to have, for your Professional and school duties . . . Amongst your friends who live respectably or amongst my relatives, ask advice as to my plan now proposed, and see if this is not right and reasonable on my part.'

Lyte's answer to this letter is not preserved, but it seems generally accepted that Mrs Lyte was very much the house manager, and her husband must have felt relieved to have such a capable deputy to free him from the worry of these day-to-day financial affairs. How could the Lytes live thus on a stipend of £134 including the newly added Queen Anne's Bounty? (Previously it had been £80 p.a. with no house or allowance). Information kindly provided by the Curator of Coutts' Museum[2] shows that the Lytes' annual income was as high as £2,800 in

[1] Letter to W. Maxwell-Lyte, 19 August (1947?).
[2] R. Brooke Caws, Curator, letter to W. Maxwell-Lyte, 28.8.1947.

1834–5 or £3,764 in 1841–2. Even on Lyte's death in 1847, after a period of heavy expenditure, his bank balance stood at £1,390. The bank records confirm that Mrs Lyte left the ultimate financial decisions to her husband, for H. F. Lyte always had the power to draw on her bank account and in September 1829 she graciously closed her account altogether, leaving all the current account income to stand in her husband's name.

It seems certain that the greater part of the Lytes' income came from the Maxwell family and estate. By taking four or five pupils at about £150 p.a. each Lyte might have increased his own income to somewhere near £700 but beyond this there was no other apparent source of funds apart from the Maxwell family. Lyte was very fortunate to have this additional income at the time of greatest need.

A sidelight into life at Berry Head, although remembered from over forty years before, is given by S. R. Hole, one-time Dean of Rochester.[1]

'I paid a visit, going with his son from Oxford, to the Rev. Henry Lyte, who was Vicar of Brixham and lived at Berryhead by Tor Bay. It was good for a young man to be in the society and under the influence of such a true gentleman, scholar, poet and saint, to be impressed by the beauty of holiness, and to be so happily assured that the voice of joy and health is in the dwellings of the righteous. He was revered by all who knew him, especially by those whose sympathies he prized the most—the poor. The fishermen came up from Brixham for supper, and sang their satisfaction in the old Devonshire chorus:

> We'll stay and have our breakfast here
> We'll stay and have a 'levener'[2] here
> We'll stay and have our dinner here
> We'll stay and have our supper here

Edmund Field, so long associated with Lancing College as Chaplain . . . was then Mr Lyte's curate.'

One cannot mention Berry Head without reference to the magnificent library which Lyte (later assisted by his son John) built up there and which in his obituary was described as 'one of the most extensive and valuable in the West of England.'[3] This was Lyte's greatest luxury and for some years two men worked full time repairing and attending to the books.[4] It was natural that a man of Lyte's interests should want to build up a library, especially in the days when it was not easy to travel to the

[1] S. R. Hole, *The Memories of Dean Hole,* 1892, pp. 75–6.
[2] i.e. elevenses.
[3] *Exeter Flying-Post,* 2.12.1847.
[4] W. Maxwell-Lyte, *British Weekly,* 3.4.1947.

more distant national and university collections. As early as November 1822, when he was at Charleton, Lyte records in one of his manuscript notebooks (a book largely made up of poems) a list of books in his library. This was somewhat short but it may not have been the full list. It contained fourteen Folio works, such as Taylor's *Hebrew Concordance,* Spenser's Works, Lyte's *Herbal,* Dodson's *Calculator,* Manby's *Statutes made under the two Charles, State Papers under Cromwell* and 26 Octavo works including Faber on the *Holy Spirit, Evangelical Magazine* (5 vols.), *Baptist Magazine* (odd volume), *Moravian Hymns,* Hall's *Sermons, Vocabular: Anglo-Saxonicum, Pensées de Rousseau,* Goldsmith's *Essays,* Watts' *Lyrics,* Addison's *Evidences* and Nollin's *Ancient History.*

Over the years, and especially during the time at Berry Head, the library grew from this modest beginning to a magnificent collection, including many rare and valuable books. Some idea of its size can be gained from an article by W. G. Hiscock, Assistant Librarian of Christ Church, Oxford[1] describing the Sale by Auction of the library by Messrs. Southgate and Barrett (often misquoted as Sotheby's) in London in July 1849. The sale, which lasted for seventeen evenings, realised £2,766,[2] an immense sum for those days, and the sale catalogue[3] ran to 296 pages. The top price (£40. 10s.) for a single book went for the 1611 edition of Robert Chesters' *Anuals of Great Brittaine,* which included Shakespeare's *Phoenix and the Turtle.* This went into Thomas Corser's library and from there in 1873 to the British Museum. The sale catalogue was prefaced as follows:

'One circumstance which tended greatly to augment the value of Mr Lyte's library was the singular advantage which his frequent journeys afforded him, of exchanging inferior copies of works which he possessed for copies in better, finer, condition. Thus he was enabled not only to select the rarest and most beautiful editions &c. of books already in his possession, but also continually to render his series of works and editions more perfect. Since the decease of the Rev. H. F. Lyte many valuable additions have been made by his son (the late) J. W. M. Lyte, Esq., who inherited his father's taste for literature, together with a more delicate taste for books remarkable for the amplitude of their margins, tall size and splendid condition.'

[1] W. G. Hiscock, *The Times Literary Supplement,* 20.6.1935.
[2] W. Maxwell-Lyte, *British Weekly,* 3.4.1947.
[3] A copy of the catalogue is available at the Devon and Exeter Institution Library, Exeter.

Hiscock states that the son's additions were for the most part new and finely bound by Messrs. Hayday and Riviere, Holborn.

The library was chiefly of Theology and old English Poetry. Mrs Hogg writes that her father had 'by his wide Bibliographical research, enriched his stores with most of the best editions of the Fathers, and (had) also accumulated a rare and valuable collection of the works of the Nonjurors, for whose quaint, severe, yet simple style, he possessed a peculiar relish, and had, at one time, partially prepared for publication, a new edition of their writings, with a history of their chief men and their times'.[1]

A letter from Sir Henry Maxwell-Lyte to Hiscock, written on 7 March 1935, states: 'My father (J. W. M. Lyte) had an income from the Maxwell Trustees which enabled him to buy books and pictures at his discretion.'[2] He also says that H. F. Lyte sold the library to J.W.M.Lyte his son. A letter which H. F. Lyte wrote to his wife from Bologna on 26 October 1846 states 'The £1,930 paid to Coutts for me is John's money for the library'—it sounds as if the money came from 'Mrs Maxwell's gift' and that J. W. M. Lyte was paying it to his father as the purchase price for the library. The library was housed in the large room at Berry Head opposite what was later called the 'Trawlers' room', Later, when the Hoggs were at Berry Head, the old library was used as a laundry, with the bookshelf marks still visible on the walls.[3]

As already mentioned Lyte added to his income by taking resident pupils at Berry Head, who were tutored along with his children by him and his curates. Lyte's letter to Mr O. Blewitt (1832)[4] mentions that 'the gentleman (sc. the Rev. J. B. Goodwin) who assists me in my ministerial work and in the education of my children has for some time past been incapacitated through illness'. Even when the Lytes were at Burton House, therefore, they were able to secure some return on the £75 p.a. Lyte had to pay Goodwin by having the children educated at home at no extra cost. The more spacious premises at Berry Head enabled Lyte to take the private pupils as well. Curate E. Wilcocks, who arrived about April 1833, assisted in this way, and the teaching staff must have been greatly strengthened by the arrival of the able J. R. Hogg as curate in Wilcocks' place about July 1835.

An insight into Lyte's character, as well as into his relationship with

[1] *Remains,* p. xxxv.
[2] Lyte family papers.
[3] John Maxwell-Lyte, letter to W. Maxwell-Lyte, 19 August (1947?).
[4] H. F. Lyte, *Commonplace Book,* p. 500.

these pupils, is given in a letter he wrote on 2 February 1833 to one of his first students, Robert Whiteway:[1]

'My dear young friend, for such I feel disposed to call you even on so short an acquaintance, I almost regretted after you had left that I had asked any terms whatever to you. The advantages of your coming to us will be all mine. Your advancement in literary attainments of every kind are considerable and my boys are so much younger than yourself that I feel indeed that we have little or nothing to impart to you but on the contrary everything to receive from you . . . My only hope is that Mr Wilcox (*sic*) whom I have written to engage may in some degree supply my deficiencies or that your most anxious desire of improvement may draw out of us more than we ever knew to be in us. At the worst should you find your hopes disappointed a removal will be practicable in the way that your letter suggests, and in the contents of that letter I shall be very happy to acquiesce . . . It will at least be my sincere desire to contribute in every way in my power to your welfare and happiness.'

Lyte goes on to ask him not to spread abroad the fact that he will charge Whiteway less than the £150 paid by the other pupil, because of the 'advantages which I anticipate to my children and myself from your residence among us'.

Some amusing comments on these students, and on their tutor the Rev. E. Wilcocks, occur in some of the letters Mrs Lyte wrote to her husband when he was away. On 29 October 1833 she wrote:

'But you are *greatly* wanted here I assure you that all things with Mr Wilcox and his pupils are very sadly at variance with what you wish. Master Pigott has not been taught a word by Mr Wilcox since I wrote last . . . Mr Wilcox is a bad example in every thing when not looked after, *believe me*—and Whiteway and Edward fall into his habits . . . as I said before you are wanted I can do very little in *your place* . . . Smoking cigars and clandestine suppers are Mr Wilcox's engagements.'

In another letter, 1 July 1834, Mrs Lyte wrote:

'If you cannot get pupils without do advertise. I think you can be more particular in your wishes by doing so and probably get better and nicer pupils. How kind Sir Harry is—I am sure he would find some if he could. There is a vast difference between Mr Kemp and Mr Wilcox—and I think a person like the former would give strong

[1] *ibid.,* p. 354.

inducements to genteel people, and it is only such that can pay well enough for you.'

Even so, Lyte's tutorial work had its finer side, especially after Hogg's arrival. Amongst Lyte's pupils was Lord Cranborne, the blind brother of Robert Cecil, who as Lord Salisbury was three times Prime Minister between 1885 and 1902. Lord Cranborne was afflicted with a form of nervous debility which, before he grew up, resulted in a complete loss of sight and general feebleness of constitution. Robert Cecil spent several holidays with his brother at Berry Head and, sixty years later, told Lady Maxwell-Lyte how lasting an impression Lyte had made upon his mind. On 3 October 1839 Lyte wrote of Cranborne to the Marquess of Salisbury: 'We were all delighted with him. Indeed, I do not think that I ever met such a promising boy, and I have no doubt of his distinguishing himself hereafter in life . . . I hope that on the whole we have returned him to Hatfield not worse for his sojourn in Devonshire, and we feel greatly obliged to your Lordship for letting us have him for so long.'[1] Lord Cranborne was mentioned in one or two of Mrs Lyte's letters to her husband; on 23 July 1838 she wrote: 'Farnham is a good boy but it is difficult to get him to read to himself—he reads to Cranborne sometimes, which is of use to both as he is a sadly incorrect reader.'[1]

Other pupils of Lyte's at Berry Head include Lord Ogilvy, son of Lord Airlie and Dick Charteris, son of Lord Elcho. The pupils occupied the east wing of the house while the family lived in the west wing.[2]

On 10 June 1834 Lyte was admitted to the *ad eundem* MA degree at Oxford. Mrs Lyte wrote to him at Oxford on 16 June saying that she hoped her husband 'would not pay too dearly for the splendid sight you witnessed either in health or pocket!'[2] A letter from Edward Hawkins, the well-known Provost of Oriel, written on 24 May 1834 to Mr Buller who had presumably enquired on Lyte's behalf, explained that as a Dublin MA Lyte could obtain the Oxford MA simply by paying a £1 fee and getting an Oxford MA graduate to present him for the degree.

The Lyte family continued to live happily at Berry Head over these years in the mid-thirties. No doubt the children were quite obstreperous; a letter from Mrs Lyte to her husband, 21 October 1833, had noted: 'The children are all of them frightfully insolent to poor Miss Bisset . . . Mary Pope says they have never treated any governess with respect—a person who was genteel and humble in manner would be necessary to form the

[1] A. C. Ellis, *loc. cit.*
[2] Lyte family papers.

manners of a gentlewoman, but our children must have a person of some firmness, method and discipline about her.' Yet the children came to no great harm, though Henry had his firework accident about this time and in July 1836 John had a nasty fall down the hatch of a Ship of War he was visiting in the bay, from which he mercifully soon recovered. A letter from Mrs Lyte to the young Henry, 23 July 1838, says: 'You do not bear moralizing well or I should ask you if you do not feel an increasing desire to improve your many privileges—I hope you do?—and reflect sometimes.'

It has frequently been stated in popular works that Lyte refused all preferment during his long stay at Brixham.[1] It is clear from the affair of the Penzance appointment that this is not strictly true, but even so we were surprised to discover from letters kindly lent to us by the late Mr J. A. Palmes[2] that in 1835 Lyte was seeking appointment as Vicar of Crediton. This was of course at the very time when the Lytes seemed to be delighted with their new home at Berry Head. Late in 1835 the living of Crediton, with its fine cathedral-like fifteenth-century church, became vacant.

The benefice was then, as now, in the gift of the Governors of the Corporation of Crediton and Lyte applied for the post. His application was supported by sixteen magnificent testimonials from people ranging from the Bishop of Exeter (Phillpotts) and the Earl of Morley to the Curate of West Teignmouth, E. R. Rhodes. They included the two Chief Magistrates Sir John Yarde-Buller and Henry Studdy, the Archdeacon of Totnes (Robert H. Froude) and Prebendary Robert Holdsworth, the weighty Vicar of Brixham.

By modern standards it seems strange that Lyte, whose brilliance was well known in Devon, should have thought it necessary to submit so many testimonials, some from relatively obscure clerics. Indeed Vicar Holdsworth remarks in his letter: 'His general character and Talents are so well known and appreciated in this neighbourhood, that were it not, that such testimonials are required on the present occasion I shd. have hesitated in giving any, only from the conviction that there was no need of any.'

Despite the weight of testimony in Lyte's favour another candidate, the Rev. Samuel Rowe, MA, was elected, which shows that Church appoint-

[1] e.g. N. Mable, *Popular Hymns and their Writers,* 2nd edition, 1951, p. 124; *Torbay and South Devon,* Ward Lock's Red Guide, 22nd edition, 1969, p. 102.
[2] Son of the Rev. J. R. Hogg's daughter Alice, who married Canon A. L. Palmes. He was therefore a great grandson of H. F. Lyte.

ments could be as extraordinary in the last century as they often seem to-day! One of the Governors, Thomas Hugo, wrote to Lyte on 10 December 1835, expressing his sorrow that he had not been chosen for the living. He wrote: 'The great impression which you made upon the inhabitants of Crediton in general will not easily be effaced. Mr Rowe's discourses, tho' little talented, appear to have been composed to excite the feelings of his audience, and were delivered with such tremendous power of voice, that a very large party was raised in his favor, and this perhaps may have influenced a majority of the Governors.'

Why should Lyte have wished to leave at this stage, when the family seemed so well settled at Berry Head? It seems unlikely that the higher benefice income of Crediton ($£425$ p.a. in 1831[1]) was the attraction, for his bank record shows that his income was $£2,800$ in the year 1834–5 and he was rich enough to send three sons to Oxford or Cambridge, to have extended tours abroad, to build up his lavish library and to afford a substantial complement of servants[2] at Berry Head. Nor would one have thought that Crediton was a more attractive situation—there was Lyte's long-standing love of the sea and his genuine devotion to the fishermen and by comparison Crediton would have seemed a dull town. Even All Saints', with all its limitations, he had described as that 'dear little church' and it seems unlikely that the superior architecture of Crediton church would have been enough to draw him away from Brixham.

We can only think of two possible reasons for the move. Mrs Lyte was always wanting to leave Brixham in her Burton House days, and it may have been that she still wanted to move, though there is no evidence of this. Secondly, although Lyte was ostensibly fairly fit, he was certainly a sick man four years later, and it may be that by 1835 he instinctively realised that the time had come to take a lighter job. It seems amazing that a man like Lyte, with such a wealth of talent and personal charm, and who moved freely amongst the upper classes, was probably never offered more than a living worth $£134$ a year. Just one of his private

---

[1] W. White, *History, Gazetteer and Directory of Devonshire*, 1850, p. 271.

[2] During repairs at Berry Head some years ago, a piece of wood was found on which apparently the whole household signed their names on 22 November 1841. The names were: Elizabeth Hockaday, William Humphreys, Lizzie Whiting, Sam[l] Shrives (coachman), William Dollon, Cecil A. Bisshopp, Anna Maria M. Lyte, W. Bourne Marsland (curate), Henry Francis Lyte, Mary Pope (nurse-maid), Anne Lyte, Grace Pearce, Priscilla Paul, Fanny Dawe. The wood now reposes in Brixham Museum. Sir Cecil Bisshopp, Bt. was Lyte's Churchwarden in 1842.

pupils paid more in fees and board than the whole benefice income! But so it was, and it is fairly certain that Lyte was not offered any preferment after 1839 because of his health.

The Crediton letters, though open testimonials which would naturally not mention anything untoward, give a valuable contemporary estimate of Lyte's qualities. We quote at length from Archdeacon Froude's letter, written from Dartington Parsonage on 7 October 1835:

'To meet the growing demand for seats (sc. at All Saints' after Lyte's arrival in 1824) it was soon found necessary to make a considerable addition to it—but being still inadequate to the increasing congregation the chapel was further enlarged in 1827. By these means and in the face of much discouragement, church room was provided for eighteen hundred persons, and under the sanction of HM Commissioners the Chapel was converted into a district church.

During the progress of the improvement my official duty on many occasions led me to witness the zealous but patient perseverance of Mr Lyte and the esteem in which he was held by the great body of his parishioners.

In this way I became acquainted with the personal sacrifices made by Mr Lyte in the way of pecuniary contributions towards the general charges of that work, and if the reports, which have reached me, are not greatly exaggerated, there is reason to believe that the whole income of his benefice would fall short of his private charities, which have been most judiciously employed in promoting the general welfare of his parishioners—among other things the establishment and support of a Sunday School where several hundred young persons are gratuitously instructed by Mr Lyte in the elements of sound religious knowledge . . . I hardly know how to express my opinion of his gentlemanly character and of those other accomplishments which have contributed to his influence with his parishioners. I must not, however, omit to mention that few, whom I have heard, excel him in the clearness and eloquence with which he enforces from the pulpit the doctrines of the Established Church.'

The Archdeacon then referred to the great difficulties of teaching the Faith in Lyte's parish, where most of the inhabitants were so occupied during six days of the week as to indispose them to receive religious instruction on the seventh; but for Lyte's exertions there might have been a systematic profanation of the Sabbath. He concluded with the words: 'I believe no-one could have discharged his duties with more fidelity and good judgement, or could have shown himself to be better suited to a large and most difficult parish.'

Space will not allow summaries of all the testimonials. Henry Studdy's letter referred to 'the moral reformation, which under God's blessing he has been the means of working in Brixham' which had become 'a very superior place to what I remember it before his residence here'. For one man to change the morals of a whole town, and a difficult town at that, was an immense achievement. The testimonial from the Rev. John Templer, Rector of Teigngrace, bears 'my very humble testimony to your entire qualification and fitness to hold not only the Vicarage of Crediton but even the Archbishoprick of Canterbury'! In general the letters praised Lyte for his indefatigable energy in visiting and every kind of pastoral work, for his Sunday Schools which were obviously regarded as a unique achievement, his very generous charitable help both to the distressed and to local church work, the 'moral reformation' which he had brought about, and his pulpit eloquence, kindness and other personal gifts.

In 1838 Lyte preached the second of the four sermons preserved in the *Remains*.[1] It is headed: 'Addressed to the Fishermen of Brixham, on the Sunday after the Coronation, 1838.' To celebrate the Queen's Coronation it had been decided that all the fishermen would have three days ashore. Much as Lyte had already done to improve the morals of the seagoing fraternity, it was widely feared that there would on this festive occasion be a great deal of drunkenness and unworthy behaviour. When it came to the time, however, the men's behaviour throughout had been excellent. Lyte had been accustomed to invite the fishermen to his church for a special sermon each year before they sailed off to Ramsgate or other distant waters for some months. Amongst the family papers is a copy of a letter, signed by both Lyte and Hogg, written on 7 November 1839 to 'The Fishermen of Brixham'. It urged them 'for the good of your souls, to come and hear a few words of exhortation, *on Sunday morning next,* before you depart from your homes, and from us . . . Come and pray that God may be with you and bless you while away, and bring you safely home again'. Once more the time had come for them to leave their homes and spend the winter off Ramsgate.

In a similar manner, this sermon had been arranged for them at the end of their three days ashore for the Coronation. The text was John 21, v. 6: 'Cast the net on the right side of the ship and ye shall find.' As in the

[1] pp. 235f.

Saltram sermon, Lyte compared the fate of a God-fearing person (in this case a fisherman) with one who turned a deaf ear to the claims of the Almighty. 'I think it seems to be now pretty generally acknowledged, that those who rob God of his holy day and employ it in secular pursuits, find their temporal interests but little promoted thereby', he continued. 'Many persons seem to wish to keep out of sight the precariousness of the sailor's life; and think it politic to maintain, that men are as safe at sea as on shore'. It was not his maxim, Lyte went on, to shut his eyes to the truth and to say 'Peace, peace, when there is no peace'. After describing in vivid terms the death of a non-believer in a storm at sea, Lyte contrasts this with the lot of a practising Christian in the same position: 'The storm may rage around him, but there is a still small voice which calms the storm within; and amidst the din of conflicting elements he is enabled to exclaim, "The Lord is my hope and strength, a very present help in trouble; therefore will I not fear, though the mountains be carried into the midst of the sea". ' It was a typical Revivalist sermon, although orna-mented by Lyte's unusual elegance of style. There is the characteristic note of fear, from which faith in God will bring complete deliverance. There was no sign at all of the Tractarian outlook which was soon to begin to influence his thought. We see Lyte here at the height of his powers, though the days of his physical decline were so close at hand.

10

DECLINING DAYS

IN 1839, when only 46 years of age, Lyte wrote his poem 'Declining Days'. It clearly refers to himself and shows that by now he knew that his days on earth were numbered. There is a very moving human pathos about the twelve verses, the first of which runs:

> Why do I sigh to find
> Life's evening shadows gathering around my way?
> The keen eye dimming, and the buoyant mind
> Unhinging day by day?

In the third verse he fears, as do so many men when death is in sight, that in a few years he will be completely forgotten.

> No! 'tis the thought that I—
> My lamp so low, my sun so nearly set,
> Have lived so useless, so unmiss'd should die;
> 'Tis this, I now regret.

In the eighth and ninth verses he hopes that before he dies he may compose a song which may be of lasting benefit to mankind, a wish which was wonderfully fulfilled during the very last few weeks of his life when he wrote 'Abide with Me'.

> But might I leave behind
> Some blessing for my fellows, some fair trust
> To guide, to cheer, to elevate my kind
> When I was in the dust,
>
> Might my poor lyre but give
> Some simple strain, some spirit-moving lay
> Some sparklet of the Soul, that still might live
> When I was passed to clay!

The poem ends with a verse of prayerful faith (v. 12):

> O Thou! whose touch can lend
> Life to the dead, Thy quick'ning grace supply
> And grant me, swanlike, my last breath to spend
> In song that may not die!

In the spring of that year, after weeks of suffering, Lyte was persuaded to see 'the celebrated Dr Chambers'.[1] A letter from Mrs Lyte, then

[1] *Remains,* p. xlii.

staying with the Hoggs near Kettering, to her husband at Brixham begins:
'I was glad to receive your last letter though very sorry to find that Doc^r
Chambers had put you to so much pain and inconvenience'. No doctor
of this name could be found in the contemporary Exeter, Plymouth and
Torbay directories, and in view of the epithet 'celebrated' we can be fairly
certain that he was Dr W. F. Chambers,[1] considered the leading physician
in London at the time, and Physician-in-Ordinary to William IV and
Victoria. Garland and Appleyard both give the physician's name as
Dr Chalmers, but this is probably due to confusion with Dr Thomas
Chalmers, the noted Scottish preacher,[2] whom Lyte mentions once or
twice in his *Book of Facts, Fancies &c.* At all events Dr Chambers warned
Lyte that 'unless he slackened his sails and cast anchor for a while, his
voyage of life would soon be over'. Yet there was no apparent disease,
and even this warning awoke no serious alarm, and he shortly returned
with renewed vigour, and unabated zeal, to his varied avocations. Thus
he continued to exhaust the remainder of his health and strength, with
but brief intervals of relaxation, in the constant drudgery of teaching,
and in parochial ministrations, or in satisfying the claims which were
largely made on his time and benevolence by the attention of friends and
acquaintances, or the importunities of all who sought and found in him a
ready friend and helper in their time of need.[3] The church registers show
that Lyte only took a baptism on one day between 6 March and 28 July
and only conducted a wedding on one day between 5 February and
21 October 1839, although he ministered fairly continuously between
January and October 1840.

At last, in the summer of 1842, Lyte was induced to spend a holiday in
Norway from which he derived much benefit. Some details of this are
recorded in letters reproduced in the *Remains,* pages lxiiif. He left Hull
at mid-day on 13 August 1839, and reached Christiansand two days later
after a very comfortable journey. On Christiansand Cathedral he commented: 'There was an altar curiously ornamented with marble figures
in alto relievo, and candles on the table. The minister also wears a stole of
rich crimson velvet and a large cross on the back of his surplice. What
will K. say to this in Protestant Sweden?'[4] The last letter quoted, dated
30 August, was from Köngsberg, Norway. Lyte was impressed with the
beauty of the country and the cleanness of their towns.

[1] *Dictionary of National Biography,* Vol. X, p. 29.
[2] *ibid.,* Vol. IX, p. 449.
[3] *Remains,* p. xlii.
[4] Norway and Sweden were united at the time.

After this he continued his work with zest, but during the autumn and winter of 1843 when he had been for some months without assistance, 'an attack of bronchitis followed his exposure to night air, and the constant exertion of his lungs; and as his symptoms during the following spring daily assumed a more formidable character, he was at length compelled to follow the advice of his medical attendants, and to seek in a warmer climate and at a distance from home, that bodily health and mental relaxation which he was unable to secure in England'.[1] The registers show that Lyte officiated continuously from 15 October 1843 until 28 January 1844; Hogg was still curate, of course, but it seems that he must have been away.

As Walter Maxwell-Lyte put it,[2] the last few years of Lyte's ministry were unhappy. This was not only because of his ill-health, but because increasing numbers of his congregation left him for the Dissenters and in particular for the newly-arrived Plymouth Brethren. One reason for this was that in later years he became regarded as a high churchman. He had certainly been influenced by Tractarian views over the last twelve years or so of his life. John Maxwell-Lyte in his letter to his brother wrote: 'H. F. L. took a prominent part in the Oxford Movement with Newman, Vaughan,[3] Manning and others—whilst they went on to Rome he remained in the Church of England.' This is almost certainly overstating the case, but we will trace as fully as possible this development in Lyte's thought. Keble's Assize Sermon had been preached on 14 July 1833; Newman's first three tracts all appeared in September of that year, being largely inspired by Richard Hurrell Froude, son of Robert H. Froude, Archdeacon of Totnes and Vicar of Dartington.

It was largely through the Froudes that Lyte was brought in touch with the Oxford Movement. Robert Froude had been Lyte's Archdeacon during all his time at Brixham and knew him very well. Hurrell his son had much in common with Lyte, being a gay, exuberant and highly intelligent young Fellow of Oriel College, a born poet (rather than a theologian) who died of tuberculosis in 1836 at the early age of thirty-three.[4] The first sign we have found of Lyte's possible interest in the Oxford Movement comes in November 1833, when Archdeacon Froude wrote to Lyte asking him to sign the Address which was presented to the

---

[1] *Remains,* p. xliii.
[2] *British Weekly,* 3.4.1947.
[3] Maxwell-Lyte seems mistaken here. Cardinal Vaughan was always a Roman Catholic and was not born until 1832.
[4] J. R. H. Moorman, *History of the Church of England,* 1953, p. 339.

Archbishop of Canterbury (William Howley) with the signatures of 7,000 clergy in February 1834. The Address, which assured the Archbishop of its supporters' 'devoted adherence to the Apostolic Doctrine and Polity of the Church over which you preside', was aimed against the threatened 'liberalising' of the Church by removing doctrinal statements from the Prayer Book and perhaps eliminating the Creeds.[1] The signatories promised the Archbishop 'the cheerful co-operation and dutiful support of the Clergy in carrying into effect any measures that may tend to revive the discipline of ancient times, to strengthen the connection between Bishops, Clergy and People, and to promote the purity, the efficiency and the unity of the Church'.

Archdeacon Froude's letter asked Lyte to confer on the subject 'with such of your clerical neighbours as you can see most conveniently' and stated that if no material objection was made the Archdeacon would put a sheet in circulation for signature in each deanery early in the following month. Lyte was thus being given a privileged position, almost as if he were Rural Dean. The Dean Rural's Visitation Book shows, however, that Lyte held this office only in the year 1829.[2] The letter concluded:

'I inclose for your acceptance a small collection of tracts which have recently been printed in Oxford. Should they meet your approbation, & you think the distribution of a few copies among your particular friends desirable—I shall be happy to furnish you with them, as well as with some others of the same character as I may have the means. You will perceive that they are written by men of no ordinary stamp and views. I need only mention the names of Keble, Newman &c.

I am my dʳ Sir yours very truly,
R. H. Froude."

Although hand-written this letter seems to be in the nature of a circular, containing no personal material at all apart from Lyte's name. The next letter from the Archdeacon in the Lyte family papers was written from Dartington Parsonage on 19 September 1835.

'My dear Mr Lyte,

We were disappointed in our expectations of a visit from Mr Newman three weeks ago, but he is now with us.

[1] R. W. Church, *The Oxford Movement*, 1891, pp. 92f.
[2] The officer was styled 'Dean Rural' in Exeter Diocese at the time.

Will you then do me the favour of meeting him one day of the coming week? Mr Twysden[1] who was once a pupil of Mr N's promised to spend a day with him whenever he might be here: I shall write to him by this post on the chance of his seeing you on Sunday & being able to name a day that will be convenient for our having the pleasure of seeing you both. I have no engagement but for Tuesday. We dine at five but shall be glad to see you at as early an hour as you can come & I hope you will be able to stay the night.

Hurrell has been very unwell since I saw you but I hope he is now getting the better of the feverishly bilious attack which weakened him very much and alarmed me exceedingly.

With kind comps. to Mrs L.

I am my d^r Mr Lyte

Yrs very truly

R. H. Froude.'

Another letter from the Archdeacon to Lyte, written from Dartington on 4 February 1837, was sent with a copy of *Lyra Apostolica,* the well-known book of religious verse by the early Tractarians, 'with which Mr Newman desired me to present you with his kind remembrance. All the poetry has appeared, as you will observe by the preface, in the *British Magazine.* Those marked β were written by Hurrell, δ is Mr Newman's work and γ is Mr Keble's.[2] The others belong to, *i believe,* Mr H. Wilberforce & Mr Williams a fellow and tutor of Trinity'. In a letter written home from Rome in December 1846 Lyte referred to 'Mr Newman, whom I knew at Oxford'. It is possible that Lyte stayed at Oxford for a while at some stage and met the leading Tractarians, though the only visit to that city of which we have found record was in June 1834 when he went to receive his Oxford MA. He may well have stayed a week or two there on that occasion; the Oxford Movement was flourishing and it would have only been natural, if Lyte had shown some interest, for Hurrell Froude to have taken him to see his Tractarian friends at Oriel and elsewhere.

Among Lyte's family papers is an interesting fragment of Dr Pusey's writing, copied in Lyte's own hand and ending: 'Signed E. B. P.' It bears no date, but its reference to the decoration of churches suggests that it is

[1] Curate of St Mary's, Brixham at this time.

[2] For a note on this system of Greek lettering, see L. I. Guiney, *Hurrell Froude,* 1904, p. xi. It is also used in Froude's *Remains* (1838), which like Lyte's *Remains* was published by Rivington.

at least as late as 1841, as does also the mention of 'Puseyism', for Pusey scarcely came into such prominence until after Newman's withdrawal in 1841.[1] The opening part of the document is as follows:

'Dr Pusey being asked by a lady to give an account of Puseyism wrote off hand the following:

It is difficult to say what people mean when they designate a class of views by my name—for since there are no particular doctrines but it is rather a temper of mind which is so designated it will vary according to the individual that uses it. Generally speaking that which is so designated may be reduced under the following heads.

1. High thoughts of the sacraments. 2. High estimate of Episcopacy as God's ordinance. 3. High estimate of the visible Church as the body wherein we are made and continue members of Christ. 4. Regard for Ordinances as directing our own doctrines and disciplining us such as daily prayers Fasts and feasts. 5. Regard for the visible part of Devotion such as the Decorations of the House of God, which act insensibly on the mind. 6. Reverence for and deference to the ancient Church of which our own Church is looked on as the Representative.'

Pusey then contrasts this with 'the system of Calvin which has been partly adopted in our Church, though not as it is for the most part held by conscientious and correct-minded persons'. The interesting part about this document is that, apart from occasional abbreviations and minor deviations, it is identical wth Pusey's statement of his doctrines published years later in Liddon's *Life of Pusey*.[2] Liddon also records that 'a lady wrote to Pusey' asking for information, but apart from this he does not seem to know the precise origin of the document. We presume that Lyte and Liddon obtained the text from a common source.

For further evidence on this development in Lyte's theology we must turn to the Memoir in the *Remains*, page xxxii. In this connection it must be remembered that the authoress Mrs Hogg herself became a 'definite Catholic' Anglican in later life, forsaking All Saints' for the 'Catholic' Mission Church of St Peter when the latter opened within All Saints' parish in 1874. So her remarks might possibly be biased; they were however written before 1850, long before her connection with St Peter's.

[1] According to H. P. Liddon, *Life of Pusey*, 1895, Vol. 2, p. 139, however, the title 'Puseyism' became popular in 1840.

[2] Vol. 2, p. 140.

Mrs Hogg states that a development in her father's religious outlook was clearly discernible in the latter years of his life. He began in the manner of the so-called Evangelical clergy. In their system 'the personal influence of the minister, rather than the legitimate authority of the Church, was the mainspring of action, and the various portions of the parochial system were carried out as the individual judgement of each Clergyman might deem best', so that there arose a fresh need for some weapons against the three-fold peril of false doctrine, heresy and schism. This need was keenly felt by Lyte, his daughter adds. She said that the people 'readily learned to turn aside from one whom they loved and honoured as a man, but in whom they failed to recognise the higher authority of a duly commissioned Ambassador of Christ'. Included in this movement was the 'wild fanaticism' of the Plymouth Brethren.

Mrs Hogg claims that in later life 'those who knew him best, will say that his love for Evangelical truth was as warm, as pure, as practical as ever; but he saw very clearly the need of combining with it that apostolical order which had been omitted in his earlier teaching' . . . (He believed in) 'the principles and practices of our own Scriptural Church against either the fallacious refuge of Rome's stagnant infallibility, or the irregularities or latitudinarianism of those who would abrogate, as heartless formality, all attention whatsoever to Church order and discipline.' Throughout his life he grew towards this position from a simpler Evangelicalism. He always had 'an entire, simple dependence on the atoning sacrifice of our blessed Lord'. Mrs Hogg drew attention to the fact that Lyte's library included many works of the Fathers and Nonjurors, and adds: 'he was led to turn his attention to the various publications of the Oxford School'.

Appleyard, page 33, comments: 'About this time (1844) he was greatly concerned on account of some divisions which had arisen in his church. Certain moderate high church practices which he introduced caused trouble, and this, together with the spread of Plymouth Brethren ideas in the town, disturbed several influential members of his congregation. Although in an extremely weak condition, he preached to his people a sermon specially designed to secure peace and unity. Happily the discourse bore speedy and satisfactory fruit before his failing health made it imperative for him to leave the sacred place in charge of others. Shortly afterwards he preached a farewell sermon prior to leaving for France and Italy.'

It is not certain what these 'moderate high church practices' were. The Dean Rural's Visitation Book shows that in 1842 the pulpit and reading desk, which had until then stood in front of the altar, were moved to the sides. This had actually been recommended by the Rural Dean at his visitation both in 1832 and 1841, but as is well-known from modern experience the Rural Dean is often kind enough to recommend changes which the incumbent tells him are desirable! Such a step was perhaps a little in advance of the times in a town especially noted for its Evangelical traditions. There is a local story, too, that at this time Lyte put a wooden cross on the altar, though we have found no written record of this. In 1829, when Lyte was visiting his own church as Rural Dean, he recommended that the Commandments be put up at the *altar*,[1] and in his letter of 21 February 1832 to Mr O. Blewitt[2] he speaks of the 'handsome altar piece' at All Saints'. The very use of the word 'altar', rather than 'holy table' or 'Communion table', at such an early date might at least show that there was another side to Lyte apart from the Evangelical fervour of his early sermons.

In addition Mrs Lyte's lack of tact and her somewhat extreme Evangelical position, not to mention her membership of the Methodist Meeting House, may have aggravated the difficulties. We may hazard a guess, too, that Lyte's long periods of absence from the church over these last years may have led to a worsening of the situation. The story of the newly-liberated African countries to-day shows how vulnerable is the position of any ruler when he is absent from his post, and experience indicates that church congregations can sometimes be callously unsympathetic towards an incumbent suffering from a long illness, as if to say that it is not fair for the vicar to draw his stipend while the curate does the work!

At all events it seems that from 1843 onwards more and more of Lyte's congregation seceded, often to the Plymouth Brethren, until in 1846 came his crowning misery, the complete desertion of his choir to the Brethren. The story is told by F. A. Jones:[3]

'Some six or seven years ago I happened to be staying in Brixham and was fortunate enough to meet a member of Mr Lyte's choir. "I was a member of Mr Lyte's choir" he said "in 1846, I and a dozen others, all dead now. We were deeply attached to him. He had the gentlest expression and the most winning manner possible, yet I suppose we gave him more grief than all his trials of ill-health. We

[1] *Dean Rural's Visitation Book*, Lower Brixham District Church.
[2] H. F. Lyte, *Commonplace Book*, pp. 500f.
[3] F. A. Jones, *Famous Hymns and their Authors*, 3rd edition, 1905, p. 12.

left his choir and gave up teaching in his Sunday School, and though I should probably do the same thing to-morrow under similar circumstances, it gives me a feeling of intense sadness even now when I think of it.

"This is how it came about. A short while before he left us to go to Nice, where it was hoped the climate would benefit his health, some influential members of the Plymouth Brethren visited Brixham and persuaded ten of us to join them. After due deliberation we went in a body to Mr Lyte and told him we intended to leave his church. He took it calmly enough, though we practically constituted his whole choir, and said that nothing would be further from his thoughts than to stand between us and our consciences. He bade us think the matter over very seriously and come to him again in a few days. We did so but our decision remained unaltered. We left him and never entered his church again. When 'Abide with Me' came to be written each of us was given a copy, and then we realised, perhaps more keenly than anyone else, the true meaning of those words 'When other helpers fail and comforts flee' ". '

Some additional information on this point comes from the letters of the Rev. G. Stuart Cann, written in 1947. He would probably have obtained his information from his father's reminiscences and from Miss Hogg, whom he knew well. He writes as follows:

'Most grievous of all to Lyte was the desertion of his "Helpers". These were 12 devout young men, belonging to some of the most respected families in the town, educated above their fellows, to whose spiritual training and welfare Lyte had specially devoted himself. Under his guidance, they had not only laboured for God in their own church, but they went out in twos and threes to the villages and hamlets around the countryside conducting simple services. My father knew 7 of these men intimately. Only one of them finally found sanctuary with the Plymouth Brethren. The others became active members of the Baptist and Congregationalist Churches. Their defection from All Saints' was a great loss and deep grief to H. F. L. to whom they owed so much.'

Most of the popular accounts of this defection from Lyte's church mention the Plymouth Brethren only, but it would have been surprising if some of them had not moved over to the strong Calvinistic Baptists (who had established themselves in Brixham fifteen years before All Saints' was built), or to Mrs Lyte's Methodists, or to the Independent

Chapel (Congregationalist) which was built in 1843, just at the time this controversy was raging. The Plymouth Brethren receive no mention at all in contemporary directories[1] whereas all these other chapels are noted.

Nevertheless, it seems from Mrs Hogg's and various popular accounts that it was mainly the Plymouth Brethren who were involved. Their first English centre was opened at Plymouth in 1830 by ex-Anglican priest J. N. Darby, who had founded the movement in Ireland a year or two before. The Brethren's rather extreme Biblical Calvinism, coupled with a Puritanical moral outlook with no organised ministry and complete autonomy of the local church, carried with it a certain amount of novelty and even excitement.[2] Whether or not it was because William of Orange first landed at Brixham in 1688, the town has always had and still has a markedly Protestant outlook and Evangelical sects have always flourished there. There is still a reasonably strong congregation of 'Open' Brethren at the Mount Pleasant Hall, Brixham, but this was not built until 1877 and it seems that the Brethren probably met in houses in Lyte's time. As Brixham and Plymouth were the chief fishing ports in Devon, it was inevitable that the Plymouth Brethren movement should spread rapidly to Brixham.

To give the clearest possible indication of Lyte's theological position at this time, we quote from two more of his letters. On 17 June 1844 he wrote to Bishop Phillpotts in answer to a query about his former curate W. Bourne Marsland.[3] 'He was when with me a deplorably low churchman, opposed even to the elementary principle of Baptismal Regeneration. His views have, I believe, been somewhat improved since he left me . . . still I fear that he is to be found among the groundlings.' Davies comments: 'The writer himself was evidently not among the "groundlings", to which category Gorham would undoubtedly have been assigned!' A month previously Lyte had written another letter to the Bishop mentioning that his new curate, the Rev. Henry Surtees, would be receiving a grant towards his salary from the Additional Curates' Society, with its Catholic background.

On the other hand Lyte wrote to his wife from Paris on 15 October 1844: 'It was gratifying to find my friend (Samuel) Wilberforce so completely removed from any of the religious extremes of the day blending in fact Evangelical doctrine with apostolical order.'[4] Wilberforce,

[1] e.g. W. White, *History, Gazetteer and Directory of Devonshire*, 1850, p. 426.
[2] *Oxford Dictionary of the Christian Church*, ed. F. L. Cross, 1966 reprint, p. 1086.
[3] G. C. B. Davies, *Henry Phillpotts Bishop of Exeter, 1778–1869*, 1954, pp. 195–6.
[4] Lyte family papers.

although an Oriel man and a great friend of leading Tractarians, had never become a Tractarian *in a partisan sense,* although doubtless he was considerably influenced by the loftier Catholic ideals. Lyte's position in 1844 must have been very similar. Whereas in the days of his Penzance sermon, denominations seemed to mean little or nothing to him, by the eighteen-forties he had become a good Anglican. He had come to love his church with its historic episcopate, sound learning and links with the ancient past. As pointed out by Newsome,[1] in the mid eighteen-thirties when the Evangelical movement appeared for a time to be a spent force, many regarded the Tractarians as the legitimate heirs of the Evangelicals, in standing for holiness and sound orthodox teaching as against what was thought to be the excessive liberalism of latitudinarians and modernists. The Tractarians had exuberant confidence and a practical programme of action; many Anglicans at this time supported them from the highest motives without ever thinking that they were indulging in any form of partisanship. Lyte in all probability was of this frame of mind.

Lyte's very last sermon at All Saints', to which reference will be made later, was on the subject of the Holy Communion, and was notable for its complete lack of partisan spirit. Indeed it was a model of Christian tolerance, devotion and holiness. Lyte said that the Holy Communion not only renewed for Christians the great sacrifice of the Cross, but it spread for them a feast of love. He saw the Eucharist as a sacrifice to God, though equally he saw it as the Lord's supper. There was an emphasis on ordinances, showing his preoccupation with law and order in the Church. In one sense, therefore, he had shifted from his earlier Evangelical position, but in another sense his Evangelical insights were still in evidence. The Tractarian influence on his thought was evident in the sermon, yet his theological position was nowhere near that of Pusey, Froude, Keble or Newman.

On 1 October 1844 Lyte preached a sermon at All Saints' just before he was due to leave for the Continent, and go on a journey from which he and many of his parishioners thought he might never return. The text was appropriately 2 Corinthians 13, v. 11: 'Finally, brethren, farewell. Be perfect, be of good comfort, be of one mind, live in peace; and the God of love and peace shall be with you.'[2] He spoke of St Paul's sorrows over the divisions of the church at Corinth, and from this he moved to the divisions in his own church. 'My dear Christian brethren, these divisions, and contentions, and schisms . . . (tell) us too plainly that . . . in spite of the

---

[1] David Newsome, *The Parting of Friends,* 1966, p. 14.

[2] *Remains,* pp. 269f.

progress that may seem to have been made of late in the circulation of scriptural knowledge, the extension of education, and the spread of the Gospel among the heathen, there is still something fearfully defective in our system—some rottenness at the core, some worm at the root of our gourd which is sure to blight and wither it in the end' . . .

'Remember that it is not party spirit, not head knowledge, not belonging to this or that body of religionists that will save you, but humble faith in the blood of Christ, and holy obedience to His blessed will. Be diligent attendants then on the means of grace; wait on God perseveringly in public and in private; keep the Sabbath holy; frequent the house of God; and, when you assemble here, think, at times, of your absent minister . . . Finally then, brethren, farewell. I cannot trust myself to say more, but be perfect, be of good comfort, be of one mind, live in peace, and the God of love shall be with you.   Amen.'

11

THE CLOSING YEARS

As EVENTS were to show, Lyte did not die on this 1844 journey but he actually lived another three years. We can trace his experiences on this journey from the *Remains* and from various of his letters home which survive. The *Remains,* page xliii, states that shortly after the sermon just mentioned 'amidst the mingled pain and comfort afforded him by the heartfelt expressions of regret from hundreds of his people, who watched his departure, he bade farewell to the happy home of many years'. On 15 October 1844 Lyte wrote home to his wife from Paris. This was only fourteen days after the sermon had been preached, so he must have left Brixham almost immediately afterwards.

The letter shows that Lyte was accompanied on the journey by his daughter Anna Maria, and by Mary Pope who for years had been the family nursemaid. He wrote that he had begun to feel the effects of 'my last terrible week at Brixham—I spat a good deal of blood daily when in a horizontal position . . . We have continued domiciled in a very comfortable hotel—where we have beautiful apartments and dine daily at the table d'hôte with 70 or 80 people'. They were travelling by railroad and steamboat and had had their passports visaed and countersigned.[1] The *Remains* account goes on to say that Lyte planned to hasten to Naples and winter there, but 'the agitation of leave-taking, and the early bleak weather which set in while passing through France, were too much for his shattered constitution, and he was more than once compelled by illness to pause in his onward course'.

By 11 November when the next available letter was written, the party had reached Leghorn (Livorno). The weather, Lyte said, was very stormy: 'I am myself too ill to move further for the present . . . after coughing up a pint or so of blood and pus I was enabled to get up.' He had met friends there, including Sir Thomas Acland. 'At present I cough violently and almost incessantly especially at night and consequently feel very weak and exhausted . . . How happy to have him (*sc.* Hogg) with

[1] Where no reference to the *Remains* or other work is given, the letters quoted have been seen in the original amongst the Lyte family papers.

you, kind and judicious as he is in all respects . . . Best regards to Yarranton.[1] I am much obliged to Priscilla[2] for the care she gives my books, doubtful as it sometimes appears whether I shall ever see them again.'

The next letter was written from Naples on 30 November. Lyte was most grateful for his wife's last letter: 'Indeed its kindness quite overcame me and made me feel ashamed of thinking for a moment that your interest respecting me was less than your letter proves it is.' Then followed another letter from Naples in which he said he was now 'really and truly better'. The letter included the poem 'Longing for Home' which he had just completed. The *Remains* comments that this poem 'touchingly tell(s) us how fondly his thoughts still turned to England, and yet his natural buoyancy and elasticity of spirit would not allow either such regrets, or the unintermitted bodily suffering and confinement attendant on his illness, to destroy his flow of cheerfulness'. During the winter he had more than one severe attack and once his life was in imminent danger. But by God's blessing and through the kindness of those who ministered to him he was restored to some measure of strength.[3]

Another letter from Naples, 27 December 1844, included some financial details. He was sending his wife £160, and John £40 for his wants at Oxford. He hoped that £105 would cover his own expenses until April: 'I know we must all live as near as we can to make ends meet.'

Lyte again wrote from Naples on 19 January 1845, his letter being reproduced in the *Remains,* page lxxvi. He had recently had another relapse: 'How it will be with me eventually, I scarcely dare to anticipate; but I much fear that I shall not see Berry-Head again. However, I can meekly bow, and say, "The Lord's will be done", and can trust in a Saviour's merits to give one of His unworthiest of creatures acceptance with God.' This strong note of faith is characteristic of Lyte's letters right to the end. Mrs Hogg records that the climate of Naples did not agree with her father, so he moved to Rome, where 'he spent three months in comparative comfort, though still in a very precarious state'. On 5 February 1845 he wrote from Naples: 'In a few days, however, we shall start for Rome', and by 16 February he was writing from the Eternal City: 'In spite of my suffering, I greatly enjoyed the journey hither', giving a vivid description of Appenine scenery.[4]

[1] The second curate, who remained at All Saints' until after Lyte's death.
[2] Presumably Priscilla Paul, footnote 2, p. 98.
[3] *Remains,* p. xliv.
[4] *Remains,* p. lxxviii.

Another letter, dated 16 April, begins: 'Praise be to God that the hand which pens this is not cold in the grave!' and describes how he was miraculously delivered from 'one of those terrible Italian fevers, that knock a man down like a bullock . . . in a few hours my life was not worth a day's purchase'. A letter written to his daughter just before this stated that a priest called Monsell was seeing him more than once a day and giving him Holy Communion.

His next letter to his wife (2 May) described a primitive operation he had to go through. 'It has been thought . . . expedient to form an issue in my poor old shattered frame . . . and a very disagreeable cold blooded operation it was—they that is Mr Babington an eminent London surgeon assisted by Dr Holland made an incision in the upper part of my left breast about an inch and a half long and half an inch deep. A few days after they planted in this fleshy furrow three peas and it has been necessary to defer our journey till this Cloaca or drain does its work. Unfortunately the operation cut a little too deeply in the middle and wounded a sinew which has caused a very sensitive spot in the issue.' It seems that this issue or opening was deemed necessary to let poisonous material escape from his chest! Lyte accepted his sufferings very bravely, however, and on 11 June he wrote from Venice giving a splendid description of the Regatta.

After that no more letters have been preserved until 17 February 1846, when Lyte wrote again from Rome. The *Remains,* page xlv, makes it clear however that Lyte spent the summer wandering through the Tyrol and parts of Switzerland, where he was joined by his sons and some English friends. He then returned to Rome for the winter. Mrs Hogg adds: 'The trying season of winter passed over without any apparent progress of disease—on the contrary, his greater measure of health gave him a wider range of enjoyment, both in social and intellectual intercourse, and in exploring for himself some of the many objects of interest so thickly strewn around him.'

Lyte's letter of 17 February found him much looking forward to his return to England in the spring of 1846. He mentions having had an interesting time discussing religion with two Roman Catholic priests, one a clever Scotchman (*sic*), Rector of the Scotch College, the other an American ex-Anglican clergyman who tried to convert Lyte 'but has now given up'! The American priest was going to England in the summer to become Chaplain to Lord Shrewsbury. Lyte often went with him, the letter adds, to the Collegio Romano and heard the theological lectures in Latin, which Lyte found hard to understand because of the Italian pronunciation. He found the lectures interesting, nevertheless, because of the immense learning displayed. They also went to the Jesuit sermons preached twice weekly, 'which are fine, rich, extempore, evangelical discourses and anything but what you would expect'.

On 28 February Lyte wrote again, mainly about the financial situation if he died. Although, unexpectedly, he had recovered sufficiently to return to Berry Head once more, he clearly saw that his earthly days were numbered. 'I shall do all that I can to preserve the land at Berryhead—or at least some part of it for the exercise of your cultural talents and propensities', he wrote to Anne touchingly. 'If I can preserve both (*sc.* the land at Berry Head and the library), the one for you and the other for John, even at the sacrifice of part of each, it will make me truly happy.'

A further letter, dated 7 March 1846, is copied in the *Remains,* pages lxxxii–lxxxiii. 'I therefore go about like a monk of La Trappe, dropping into bookshops and libraries . . . You would be surprised to hear what folios I have perused since I came to Italy . . . It is a great privation to me, that I cannot write. The labour of composition I find makes me ill, and the act of stooping over paper, for the purpose of writing, likewise pains and injures me. However, I have abundant reason for thankfulness that I am as I am.'

In April or May 1846 Lyte was back in England; no letters covering this journey seem to have survived. A note in the *Western Luminary,* 12 May 1846, stated that Lyte had 'recently' returned from the Continent. It added:

'The Rev. gentleman was on his appearance at Church greeted with a warmth and cordiality of feeling by his parishioners, which showed how deeply they were attached to him. Few ministers of Christ have more truly devoted themselves to the duties of the sacred office than the Incumbent of Lower Brixham. The poor and afflicted have ever found in him a ready and affectionate friend; his ear has been at all times open to their distresses, and liberally has he supplied their necessities . . . The moral and intellectual advancement of the town, was among the first objects of his solicitude, and at an immense expense he established a library, for the improvement of all, a small charge per year only being made, to keep the books in a state of repair, and fit for general use. By a series of disinterested acts, he has endeared himself to all, and the most lively anxiety prevails, that his restoration to health may be permanent. He has not yet resumed his wonted duties, and it is thought more prudent by his medical advisers, that he should, for a short period, abstain from any exertion which may too highly task his physical strength.'

The *Remains,* page xlvi, states that Lyte had hoped to superintend, if not take an active part in, his parish work. In fact, however, 'he was obliged to confine his exertions to a little private intercourse with his parishioners, and to look forward to a further exile from the colder shores of England'. None the less during this summer he prepared an edition of the poems of Henry Vaughan, which he had hoped to make the first of a series on the earlier English poets. The work included a memoir on Vaughan, and to obtain material for this he actually toured the Usk valley, where this poet had lived, during those few months.[1] Lyte felt that Vaughan had escaped proper notice owing to the 'taste for French correctness' which was in the ascendancy when the principal collections of the British poets were made.[2]

On 24 June 1846 Lyte's daughter Anna Maria was married at All Saints' to his senior curate and successor as Incumbent, John Roughton Hogg. Lyte signed as a witness but the ceremony was conducted by the Rt Rev. W. H. Coleridge, formerly first Bishop of Barbados and the Leeward Islands, to whom Hurrell Froude had for a short while acted as Chaplain. Some idea of Lyte's popularity at the time, even though this was the very year in which his choir deserted to the Plymouth Brethren, can be gained from this newspaper account:[3]

'At an early hour on Thursday the people of this town were on the *qui vive* anxiously awaiting the arrival of their beloved Pastor and his amiable daughter, whose marriage . . . took place on that day, the shops & houses were adorned with flags, ribbons and flowers, upwards of a thousand of the inhabitants thronged the area around the Church. On the doors being opened there was a rush, the aisles and seats were filled in a moment by men, women and children . . . The harbour presented a gay appearance: streamers floated from every vessel. The tars were not backward in testifying their joy at the happy event. On the following day 63 poor persons were regaled with a sumptuous dinner by the Rev. H. F. Lyte at Berry House. It is impossible to describe the interest manifested by the inhabitants on the occasion of the marriage of the Rev. gent's daughter; it may

[1] H. F. Lyte, *Sacred Poems and Pious Ejaculations by Henry Vaughan, with a Memoir,* 2nd edition, 1858, p. xv.
[2] *ibid.,* p. xiii.
[3] *Western Luminary,* 30.6.1846.

be easily conjectured, however, when it is recollected that during a residence of more than twenty years, he has endeared himself to them by the exemplary discharge of his duties as a minister, and by his kindness, benevolence, and urbanity as a gentleman.'

On 31 August 1846 the Bishop of Exeter granted Lyte official leave to be absent from the parish, because of his ill-health, until 31 December 1847. Before the end of August he had in fact left again for Italy. He planned to tour some of the old towns of Lombardy and then to winter in Rome. According to the *Remains,* pages xlvii and xlviii, the long evenings on this journey were necessarily spent in his rooms but were happily enlivened by the visits of friends and by the study of rare old folios which he could not have seen elsewhere. He enjoyed searching the libraries of all the towns he passed through. A friend said of him at the time 'I have often been struck by the exceeding resignation and cheerfulness with which he bore all his sickness, and the remarkable manner in which he was always enabled to steer clear of every thing like egotism—sickness has an almost inevitable tendency to make persons egotistical and full of morbid self-consciousness: this, however, was never his case . . . Nothing but the power of the Holy Spirit, acting on a peculiarly fine character by nature, could have produced such a result.'

A number of letters covering the journey still survive, from which we endeavour to reproduce the most significant passages. The letters make it clear that Lyte travelled up to London with his son John and their servant Mary Pope. They stayed in town at Mrs Craigie's, John's future mother-in-law, and left her by omnibus for Blackwall at 8 a.m. on Thursday, 21 August. John then returned home, while Lyte and Mary Pope embarked on the S.S. *Wilberforce* for Antwerp. The first letter Lyte wrote to his wife, before they had got to London, said: 'and now my dear how shall I thank you as I ought for all your love and tenderness to me through all my long illness?' Another letter, written on 20 August from London, mentioned that he had not received a letter from his wife; he feared that she was poorly, as she was when he left her: 'Do, my dear, dear wife take care of yourself if you have any love for me—if you have any hope of my return preserve your own health and strength to be to me what you have been all the time of my sojourn at Berry Head this summer.'

Lyte's first letter from abroad was written at Louvain on 23 August. Sir Thomas and Lady Acland had also been on board the ship. Sir Thomas, hearing Lyte coughing in the night, got out of bed more than once and asked if he could help him. Lyte could not sleep a bit. They had arrived at Antwerp at 8 a.m. on 22 August and stayed the night there. The next day they took the 9 a.m. train for Cologne, breaking their journey at Louvain. Lyte hoped to 'lose' his friends: 'I find it in fact impossible to be with others without suffering from it.' The next day they continued their journey, via Cologne, Coblentz, Mannheim, Heidelberg, Strasbourg, Basel and Zürich to Como.

He wrote from Como on Sunday, 7 September. He and Mary Pope had just been to a service with 'our beautiful Liturgy'. He had felt his eyes and heart fill in repeating the thanksgiving, for the 'mercies and blessings we were now enjoying'. After a long and fatiguing journey over the Alps he was 'well and comparatively strong'. He had been very disappointed to find the post office closed on arriving at Como, but 'at 9 o'clock this morning I was the first, and not an unsuccessful, applicant'. They had had a very rough railroad journey to Cologne, followed by a pleasant steamer trip on the Rhine to Coblentz. The next day they had gone on to Frankfort, and thence by rail to Basel. From there they had completed the journey to Como, via Zürich and the Splugen Pass, by diligence and by hired carriage. Lyte had been studying John's Homoeopathic book to find a cure for his illness.

On 16 September he wrote from Vicenza: 'I have been pursuing my intention of zigzagging about among the fine old cities of Lombardy, and they have in no respect disappointed my expectations.'[1] The next letter came from Verona on 5 October. He had been very unwell and unable to write before. The Homoeopathic medicines had had no effect, 'chiefly I suppose from my ignorance in the mode of using them. I was in consequence obliged to resort to the old treatment of blistering and bleeding, calomel and tartar emetic and seem to have had recourse to them just in time to save my life.' He had been in bed a week. He had met a splendid physician there, the Head of the local Hospitals: 'I would rather be under him than any doctor in Rome that I know of.'

His next letter, from Milan on 12 October, is quoted in the *Remains,* page lxxxv: 'For the next month we shall, I hope, be on the move, exploring the cities on the south of the Po; Piacenza, Parma, Reggio, Modena, Bologna, Ravenna &c. I have been so highly interested with my Lombardie trip . . . The old towns of Lombardy turned out to be by far the cleanest, brightest and most interesting places I have seen in Italy.' Lyte praised the churches, buildings and pictures he had seen.

[1] *Remains,* p. lxxxiv.

On 26 October he wrote from Bologna. He had been ill at Parma but was now better. He was anxious about family finances, especially as the bad weather would have affected the output of Berry Head Farm. 'I wish indeed with you that the land was our own again'—the letter sounds as if they had previously purchased the farm outright but had later had to take out a mortgage on it. He said that they both ought to save every shilling they could.

By 25 November he was writing from Rome: 'After long wanderings, much of toil and sickness, here I am once more, through Divine mercy, in a quiet resting place, for some months to come . . . I find Rome much altered I mean as to the prevailing tone of feeling. (Pope Pius IX had just succeeded to the Vatican on Gregory XVI's death, and had been enthroned on 8 November). The old "semper eadem" system has gone altogether, under the auspices of the new Pontiff, and improvement is the order of the day in all things *but one*. They diligently adhere to usage in ecclesiastical matters, but in all others the question is who can go fastest in the road of amelioration.' Lyte then mentions improvements in railroads, schools and laws; the latter is quoted in the *Remains,* page lxxxviii.

When Lyte next wrote on 7 December he had just recovered from 'severe asthmatic symptoms'. He had called in Dr Deakin who 'tried various antispasmodics internally, and at last seemed to find an efficient one in Prussic Acid of which I have taken large doses up to this time'! He mentions a *faux pas* which Newman, now a Roman Catholic and studying quietly at the College of the Propaganda in Rome, had just made. In a funeral address for a Miss Bryant a day or two previously Newman had given 'great offence' by some of his similes. 'He had likened the English running in and out of the churches to dogs going about to find their masters, and asked whether while fluttering round the true Church like moths around a candle, they did not expect to be scorched by the flames.' In a letter to his daughter on 18 December Lyte added that Newman had got into 'sad disgrace' through this, his first public address in Rome: 'The Pope is much displeased and says it is not "Aceto" but "Miele" which is suitable to such discourses!' In another letter to Mrs Hogg, undated but written in the spring of 1847, Lyte announced that Newman's destiny was settled; he was joining the Philipines, or priests of the Oratory.

This latter correspondence gives an interesting sidelight into Lyte's views on the Jerusalem Bishopric. He wrote: 'What has Bishop Daly been doing in Ireland? Re-ordaining for his own Diocese a man from the so-called Bishop of Jerusalem—What an offence against all Canonical law this re-ordination! and what an evasion of the Act of Parliament which forbad men thus ordained in the East from serving here as clergymen here at home!—I hope someone will take the matter up and trounce this outrage of all Ecclesiastical order.' Lyte shows more Catholic views on this point than Samuel Wilberforce, who approved of the Jerusalem Bishopric.

Although within a year of his death, Lyte spent an exceedingly interesting time, as his letters show, during this last spell in Rome which lasted from November 1846 until May 1847. He had his own apartments at 26 Via Gregoriana and had a manservant named Raniero to cook for him, as well as the services of Mary Pope. He much enjoyed his diet, which included woodcock, wild duck and other game with 'beautiful' butter, milk and eggs. At first he appreciated his rooms which were in the best part of the city, in a quiet and sunny position with no stairs. He did add that the smells were not very agreeable, the rooms not very clean, and although it was comfortable, the word 'comfortable' had to be understood in a very modified sense when one was abroad! Later, however, he became dissatisfied with his apartments, probably because of the hotter weather, and in April 1847 he wrote that he was anxious to get away from the city and these lodgings: 'any change, would, I think, be for the better.'

His health had its ups and downs. On 17 January he had written that he was surprisingly well. All asthmatic symptoms had gone, he could walk about with ease, go up the steepest hill and mount the loftiest staircase, eat well, sleep well, no cough and daily gaining in strength. He could now look forward with confidence, 'feeling that my complaints are not, as I had long thought them, utterly incurable'. But by 7 February he had to report: 'My old symptoms have returned and I have been confined (chiefly to bed) for the last ten days.' By 29 April he was writing: 'All Sunday and Monday week I seemed to be dying, and though I have rallied I am still very weak and ill—my pulse does not go down and intermits, and I cough incessantly day and night.' The winter had been very trying, with extremes of cold and warmth. He was immensely grateful to Mary Pope for her nursing: 'no language can express sufficiently what I owe to Pope's indefatigable attention by night and day.' In March 1847 he wrote that he had only been in the streets of Rome five times during the whole winter, and that for only four weeks of the last seven months had he been free from severe illness. None the less he took the keenest interest in all that was going on in Rome, and he was fortunate to be visited frequently by a good many friends from the sizeable English community in Rome at the time. Remarks in his letters vary from theological comment and literary criticism to some chatty bits of news to his daughter about current flirtations in Rome, especially at the dances held by Lord Ward every Thursday and Saturday.

Often, of course, domestic matters come into the correspondence. Lyte was very anxious about his daughter's first confinement, and was delighted when she was safely delivered of a daughter on 25 March 1847. 'Strange to say I could not sleep on the night of the 24th and had a strong presentiment that the confinement wd. be on the 25th—they say here the child ought to be called Mary, being born on Lady Day.' And so she was; she was baptised Mary Maxwell by her father at All Saints' on 25 April. In another letter written that April Lyte had concluded: 'a thousand kisses (I know you wd. have no objection to giving every one of them) to the dear Babe.'

Sad to say Mary only lived to the age of sixteen but her four younger sisters all survived.[1]

Lyte continued to praise the new Pope. In a letter quoted in the *Remains,* page xcviii, he says: 'He has given more than 400 £ out of his narrow income (not 25,000 £ a year) for the poor Irish'—this was just after the Potato Famine. Another letter adds: 'The Pope is receiving golden opinions from all quarters—he is everywhere reforming abuses. The other day he turned up unostentatiously in a parish church and took a service—he has preached more than any Pope for 100 years.' Another letter given in the *Remains,* page civ, states that he was as dissatisfied as ever with the Roman Catholic religion; he said that Anglicans attracted by Rome find, with Hamlet, that it is better 'to bear the ills we have, than to fly to others we know not of'. His letters were full of affection for the family; one begins 'My own dearest Anne' and sends love to, amongst others, Henry and his wife, showing that Henry's runaway marriage had already been forgiven.

Lyte's poetical inspiration and intellectual gifts were virtually unaffected by his illness. In March 1847 he wrote at Rome 'The Poet's Plea'.[2] One of the most classic of all his poems, it speaks of the rôle and mind of the poet himself. More moving, perhaps, if a little less accomplished, is the poem 'January 1st 1847', written on or about that date.[3] A poem of over

[1] Details from the Lyte Family Bible at All Saints', Brixham.
[2] *Remains,* p. 100.
[3] *Remains,* p. 93.

100 lines it began by recalling all the delights of the year that had just passed, contemplated the death which he felt lay only a little way ahead, and looked forward to union with God in heaven.

> The close! The close! How like a death-knell seems
> That solemn word to wake me from my dreams!
> One little year, yea, less than one like this,
> May bring me to the close of all that is.

sounds one verse solemnly, the last two lines of the poem ending on a note of faith:

> Be mine with Him to walk, on this depend,
> Then come what may, it all to good must tend.

The time drew near for Lyte to spend his last summer in England. He was very anxious to be home for his fifty-fourth birthday on 1 June, and above all to see his new grandchild. In a letter of 7 April he was already making plans to return to Italy the following winter. He hoped to go to Palermo and thought that his son John and Emily (soon to be John's wife) could accompany him. With Lyte's experience John and Emily could live as cheaply in Italy as anywhere, and there was no obstacle to their coming. 'John will hardly take to farming and wd., I fear be sure to lose by it, and his prospects of a librarianship are hardly bright enough to warrant his staying in London to look after this.' If John and Emily did not come, Mary Pope would be left on her own if anything happened to Lyte. In the same letter he said that he hoped to start his journey for Marseilles, en route for England, on 28 April: 'already do I long for a cut of some good English mutton, and shall relish, as you know I did last year, a good roast leg above all things.'

Unfortunately, however, Lyte had a serious relapse in mid-April. At first he thought he would never return home, but after a long consultation with his doctors he wrote on 1 May saying that he would try to make the journey. He felt he would only make it, though, if John left home at once and met him at Marseilles to 'assist Pope in the task of carrying his old father to England'. After a terrible heat-wave, with a temperature of 88° in the shade for his last ten days in Rome, Lyte just managed to get away. He was so ill that he could hardly put one foot in front of another, or draw two successive breaths without coughing a spasm. He and Mary Pope travelled the sixty miles of very rough road to Civita Vecchia by carriage: 'Many, many times did I seem to be breathing my last.' They had to wait a day or two for the steamer to Marseilles; when they arrived at the latter town on 22 May, John had not yet reached there, so they hoped to meet him at Avignon the next day. By the time John got to Avignon Lyte had already left, however, so John turned back and caught up with his father at Valence. 'His presence is a great comfort', Lyte added gratefully.

Three letters describe his journey across France. Never before or after, even on his last journey in the autumn of 1847, had Lyte been so ill on his travels. On this journey alone Lyte's letters contain no records of interesting conversations or fine buildings seen, let alone visits to libraries. His one thought, to judge from the letters, was whether he could ever manage to reach England alive. To add to his distress he caught 'a kind of "English cholera"' necessitating several days' stay at Valence, and after sailing from there to Lyons and proceeding by a 'wretched' railroad journey to Roanne, the party was delayed again because the Loire was too low to be navigable, and then through a series of accidents they missed the steamer for Orleans and had to spend five days at Nevers, where on 3 June Lyte wrote the last letter on this journey which survives. They proposed to complete their journey via Paris, Havre, Southampton and direct to Berry Head by 'the old Brunswick' coach.

The next news we have of Lyte is on 24 June, when he officiated at the marriage of his son John to Emily Jeannette Craigie, daughter of Lt-Colonel John Craigie of the Bengal Army, at St George's, Hanover Square. The *Remains* states, page 1, 'He reached England much reduced in strength, and still more shaken in his whole system. Yet the wonderful elasticity of his spirits buoyed him up, and he was able each day, more or less, to enjoy the familiar, but beautiful, scenery around his chosen haunts, and once again, with affectionate delight, to take his place in the social circle, and by his cheerful tone and Christian spirit to diffuse the happiest influence over this brief period.' Mrs Hogg states that Lyte first gave a short time to friends at a distance before returning to Brixham. Appleyard, page 45, says that Lyte was now slightly improved in health and that during this time he welcomed All Saints' Sunday School to the grounds of Berry Head where they sang some of his hymns.

Walter Maxwell–Lyte states that Mrs Lyte was away 'for some weeks' during her husband's last spell at Berry Head.[1] If this is so it is probable

[1] Letter to the Rev. D. L. Graham, 8.3.1948 (Portora papers).

that she and her daughter visited the Hoggs at Kettering to show them the new baby. In a letter from Rome on 18 March 1847 Lyte had written 'The proposed trip to Northamptonshire could best be made after my arrival'. It may seem hard for Mrs Lyte to have left her husband at this stage, but Lyte had had so many escapes from death before that his wife may well not have realized how near his end was to be.

12

LAST DAYS AT BERRY HEAD, AND THE WRITING OF 'ABIDE WITH ME'

ACCORDING to the *Remains,* pages l–li, Lyte spent his last few weeks in Brixham walking or browsing in his favourite spots—the garden at Berry Head, the library and the parish, quite enjoying himself as he reflected on the happy days that he had spent there in past years. Late in the summer, however, he had a very serious attack of inflammation 'which increased with such dangerous rapidity, that his life was despaired of: yet, even here, the merciful providence of God could be traced, in the unmistakeable evidence . . . that God's Presence was indeed abiding with him—that He would "be his guide even unto death"'. He recovered from this attack, though he was still frail. Garland, page 46, says his recovery was 'miraculous'.

Continuing the story, the *Remains* states: 'The summer was passing away and the month of September (that month in which he was once more to quit his native land) arrived . . . his family were surprised, and almost alarmed, at his announcing his intention of preaching once more to his people . . . He did preach, and, amid the breathless attention of his hearers, gave them the Sermon on the Holy Communion . . . He afterwards assisted at the administration of the Holy Eucharist, and though necessarily much exhausted, by the exertion and excitement of this effort, yet his friends had no reason to believe it had been hurtful to him.[1] In the evening of the same day he placed in the hands of a near and dear relative the little hymn, "Abide with me", with an air of his own composing adapted to the words. Within a few hours after this, the little party, consisting of his second son, his wife and a valued attendant, set out on their journey towards the genial south; a journey which he never completed, but which was ended by his peaceful entrance into that "rest which remaineth for the people of God".'

This passage requires a few comments. The date of the last sermon is a little uncertain; the *Remains,* page 281, gives 4 September but this was a

[1] Garland, page 47, states (probably correctly) that J. R. Hogg took the rest of the service.

Saturday. The true date must have been 5 or 12 September. On the whole the former seems more likely.[1] Lyte's final diary shows that he left London for the Continent on 1 October, but when did he leave Brixham? Accepting 5 September as the date of the last sermon, the *Remains* account suggests that he left on Monday, 6 September, only a few hours after the sermon was preached. Appleyard merely repeats Mrs Hogg's account, including the incorrect date (4 September) for the last sermon. Garland, page 48, states without quoting his evidence that Lyte left Brixham on Monday 13th and stayed with Julia (see below) for a few days before going on to London. Walter Maxwell-Lyte[2] writes very categorically: 'But they did not leave (Brixham) until 14 September; she (*sc.* Mrs Hogg) did not remember.'

However all these authors were wrong as to the date of Lyte's leaving Brixham, for the weekly *Western Luminary* of Tuesday, 21 September 1847 (a study of several issues strongly suggests that the Brixham local correspondent sent in his news to this Exeter paper the Saturday before) stated that Lyte's departure for Italy 'which was fixed for this week' (probably the week beginning 12 September) had been delayed because of his 'serious indisposition', but 'we are glad to say that the last two days' (17 and 18 September?) reports of him are more favourable'. The following week's issue, Tuesday, 28 September, stated 'The Rev. H. F. Lyte left Brixham yesterday morning for Italy', under the local column for Brixham. If Lyte *did* leave Brixham as late as 27 September his journey must have been uncomfortably rushed for a sick man, for he left London for Folkestone four days later. So it seems possible that the local correspondent wrote this, say on Saturday, 25 September, and meant that Lyte left on 24 September. He would not have left Brixham on a Sunday.

So although Mrs Hogg wrote the *Remains* only three years after the events happened, the date she gives for her father's leaving Brixham for the last time was between two and three weeks too early! It is fascinating to guess how she could have made this mistake; probably we shall never know the answer. Returning to her account of Lyte's departure, she correctly states that he was accompanied on the journey by his son John,

[1] Garland, p. 47, states that it was the custom at All Saints' to have Holy Communion on the first Sunday of the month, which supports the former date. The service would probably have been Mattins, Litany and Holy Communion; Garland states, p. 48, that the Holy Communion service *followed* Lyte's address.

[2] W. Maxwell-Lyte, *Western Morning News,* Exeter, 16.9.1947.

John's wife Emily (not his own wife Anne, as Appleyard wrongly states) and the 'valued attendant' who was of course Mary Pope.

The sermon, on the Holy Communion, has been mentioned above, page 113. Referring to our Lord's atoning sacrifice as being a 'pillow of consolation' to a dying soul, Lyte added 'O brethren, I can speak feelingly, experimentally on this latter point; and I stand up here among you seasonably to-day, as alive from the dead'. Although the sermon was shorter than usual, and perhaps a little quieter in tone than his earlier addresses, all Lyte's old theological ability was still there and it was a worthy conclusion to his preaching days.

We now come to the question of the exact date of 'Abide with Me'. Needless to say the hymn is surrounded with legends, and already during the present writer's time at Brixham two different visitors have each claimed that 'Abide with Me' was written for an ancestor of theirs! For a long time the universal tradition, which had somehow been passed down the Lyte family itself, was that Lyte composed the hymn within a few minutes, in a flash of inspiration during the time spent in his study at Berry Head on the afternoon of the Sunday of his last sermon, after he had strolled in the grounds of the house and watched a beautiful sunset over Torbay .This idea remains popular in many quarters, even though Garland and Appleyard both more or less refuted it many years ago. Perhaps the sheer picturesqueness of this theory makes popular writers reluctant to drop it! As late as April 1947 Walter Maxwell-Lyte favoured it in his *British Weekly* article, quoting the remarks of Charles Potter, a young gardener at Berry Head in Lyte's day who lived to a ripe old age. Maxwell-Lyte also mentions that Dr Bartlett, a grandson of Lyte's organist Mr Edward Clarke, who was still alive in 1947, claimed that Lyte sent a manuscript copy of 'Abide with Me' to Mr Clarke asking him to set it to music.[1] Bartlett said: 'The tradition, as I have always understood it, is that Mr Lyte wrote the hymn immediately on his returning home after conducting his last Sunday service at the Church prior to leaving for Nice.'

There were also several theories that Lyte had written the hymn years before his death. John Maxwell-Lyte in his letter to his brother wrote: 'H. F. L. in fact started writing the hymn when he held a curacy in Cornwall. He kept adding more verses to it and altering those he had

---

[1] The only organist mentioned in the Vestry Book in Lyte's time was, however, Mr Samuel Martin. It is widely accepted, as claimed in the *Remains,* that Lyte himself wrote the original tune.

already written. He did make a fair and final copy of it the evening before he left Berry Head for the last time.' Another widely-reported story was that Lyte had written the hymn in Wexford in 1820 after he had attended the death-bed of his friend William Augustus Le Hunte. Thus no less an authority than Dearmer quoted, obviously with full approval, Canon T. H. Bindley's letter to *The Spectator* published on 3 October 1925 which stated that the hymn was written in 1820 when Lyte was staying with the Hores at Pole Hore, near Wexford. 'He went out to see an old friend William Augustus Le Hunte who lay dying and kept repeating "Abide with me". After leaving the bedside Lyte wrote the hymn and gave a copy to Sir Francis Le Hunte, William's brother, amongst whose papers it remained. These details were given me some years ago by Sir George Ruthven Le Hunte, grandson of William Augustus, and I have had them confirmed by members of the family.'[1] Another variant was that the dying priest[2] uttered the words 'Abide with me' and that then or shortly afterwards Lyte wrote the hymn around them.

In his *Times* article of 1 November 1947, however, Walter Maxwell-Lyte expressed completely different views. He dismissed out of hand the Le Hunte theory; he had seen the copy of 'Abide with Me' belonging to the Le Hunte family. It was not in Lyte's handwriting at all, but in someone else's, and it bore internal evidence of being copied in 1847. Maxwell-Lyte thought it was probably a copy of Lyte's hymn made by a Sunday School teacher.[3]

Maxwell-Lyte also dismissed the theory, which he himself had held up to a few months beforehand, that Lyte wrote the hymn on the Sunday afternoon of his last sermon at All Saints'. This was largely because in the meantime he had come across the Julia letter. This was a letter which Lyte had written to his friend Julia from Berry Head on 25 August 1847. The last sheet of the letter was later found and is in the possession of Lyte's descendant Mr A. B. Palmes of Chagford, Devon; we have seen it in photo-copy. The first part of the letter was published in the *Remains,* page cvii, and by putting the two parts together Walter Maxwell-Lyte was able to reconstruct the original letter, for the first half of the last

---

[1] As quoted by P. Dearmer, *Songs of Praise Discussed,* 1933, p. 233.

[2] See above, page 17.

[3] According to Walter Maxwell-Lyte's notes the text of this copy was the same as that of the 'original' version except that it had 'leave' for 'left' in v. 5, line 3, and 'Shine' for 'Speak' in v. 8, line 2.

paragraph appears both in the *Remains* extract and on the last sheet of the original.

Beginning 'My dear Friend', Lyte wrote that he was meditating flight again to the south, as the signs of autumn were at hand. 'I am, therefore, calculating, with many a Deo Volente, on taking up my staff in rather less than three weeks from the present time.' Lyte continued that he hoped to reach the south of France early in October, and later to stay at Naples for a few weeks. He then planned to go on to Palermo and remain there until February 'when we might, if all are spared, return to Italy again, and get up to Rome for the spring season'.

'Such is a sketch of my plans', the letter continues, 'How small a part of them may we be permitted to carry into execution! and yet it is right to form them, while we leave the rest to Him who does for us better than we could do for ourselves. O for more of entire dependence on Him! entire confidence in Him! Not, I hope, that I am quite without these, but I want to feel them more a living principle of action. Conformity to the will and image of the Lord is no easy attainment, and it takes much hammering to bend us to it. I send you while on this subject a few lines that may interest you, as my latest effusion. By the way I still calculate on taking a bed at your house on my way to Town[1] about the 14th or 15th. Meanwhile give me a line—and believe me ever, dear Julia, your affte. friend

H. F. Lyte'

Lyte's 'latest effusion' was the hymn 'Abide with Me'! It was written in full at the end of the letter, immediately following his signature. This shows fairly conclusively that the hymn was written in July or August 1847; otherwise the term 'latest effusion' could scarcely have been used. Walter Maxwell-Lyte, having discovered this document unexpectedly, was rather at a loss to say who Julia was. In the *Times* article he said that she was most likely to have been Eleanora Julia Bolton, who later married Lyte's son Farnham and was living near Taunton in 1847. He never proved this point as far as we know, however, and Garland writes so knowingly that she was Julia Barlow, the daughter of the retired business man Lyte stayed with at Bristol before going to Marazion, that we are inclined to accept that he had special information on this point.[2]

[1] Lyte had stated earlier in the letter that he would be accompanied by John, Emily and Mary Pope on this journey abroad.

[2] There is no mention of Julia's father in *Matthews's Bristol Directory* for 1805 or 1820, however, though this only listed tradesmen and professional men, not private residents.

Whilst not revealing his sources Appleyard, pages 51–2, gives the most satisfactory account as far as the three *books* on Lyte are concerned. He agrees that Lyte gave Mrs Hogg a copy of the hymn, along with his own tune to it, in the evening of the Sunday of his last sermon, having strolled in the gardens of Berry Head in beautiful weather during the afternoon. The tune, Appleyard says, 'obviously had been written before that eventful day.' Those who knew most of Lyte 'were not sure when he commenced the hymn, or how long it took him to compose it . . . It was certainly written, in part, at least, a considerable time before that final Sunday in England'. He 'revised and partly rewrote it during the evening of that day, but did not give it its final form until he sent it home to Mrs Lyte, with possibly some verbal alterations, from Avignon (i.e. on his last journey). It certainly was not the result of swift and sudden inspiration, produced in a short space of ecstatic exaltation'. Garland, page 48, also says that the final copy of the hymn was sent home from Avignon, as indeed does Miss A. M. M. Hogg in her letter to Miss Hunt written in 1925. This is probably correct, though the extracts from Lyte's letters sent home from Avignon on 19 and 20 October 1847 given in the *Remains,* pages cviii–cx, do not mention the hymn, neither does the original of the former letter, which we have seen. There would have been no need to mention it if the text of the hymn had been enclosed with the letter.

Appleyard also states, page 50, 'A Brixham lady, Miss S. G. Jarmond, transposed, at Mr Lyte's request, the tune which he had composed . . . She was his Sunday School Superintendent, and headmistress of the day school'.[1] Appleyard adds that Lyte gave Miss Jarmond handwritten copies of some of his hymns, including 'Abide with Me', when he was about to leave for France. On page 57 of his book he says that 'Abide with Me' was sung on Berry Head lawn, in the presence of many friends, by the Brixham children for Lyte's farewell, and that it gave him unutterable joy. Several ex-Sunday School children, Appleyard says (page 58), had declared that 'Abide with Me' was well-known to them *before* Lyte left Brixham.

Garland, page 47, mentions the Julia letter, quoting the description of the hymn as 'my latest effusion'. He adds: 'It was after this illness (*sc.* the serious relapse at the end of the summer of 1847) that he wrote the

---

[1] *Pigot & Co.'s Directory* (of Devon and other counties), 1844, confirms, in the article on Brixham, that Mr Wm. King was Master, and Miss Sarah Jarmon (*sic*) was Mistress, of the National School.

famous hymn' and 'he had written the hymn on one of those evenings as he had sat quietly in meditation in his favourite retreat, but some slight revision was necessary.' Apart from the story of Lyte handing a copy of the hymn and tune to the near and dear relative on the Sunday of his last sermon, the only evidence given in the *Remains* (though this is important) is that the text of the hymn as printed there, on page 121, bears the note 'Berryhead, September 1847'.

Walter Maxwell-Lyte in the *Times* article states: 'It is, of course, impossible that he could have used this expression (*sc.* 'my latest effusion') unless the hymn had been composed very recently, and there appears to be no doubt that it was written during Lyte's last visit to Berry Head in the summer of 1847—probably in August, or possibly in July, of that year.' In another article[1] he had given the same opinion, and pointed out that Lyte had modified the words of the hymn once or twice, 'Speak through the gloom', for example being changed to 'Shine through the gloom' in the latter part of August 1847. (In the Julia letter Lyte first wrote 'Speak' for this verse, and altered it to 'Shine' with his pen). In a letter to *The Times*[2] he states that Lyte sent the manuscript to his organist Mr Edward Clarke to have the tune harmonised; this is a variant on Dr Bartlett's story, given above, that Clarke was asked to set the words to music, but it seems almost universally accepted that Lyte wrote the original tune himself.

We must now turn to the internal evidence. First, the whole tone of the hymn points to a rapidly approaching death: indeed it has often been said that 'Abide with Me' is much more of a funeral hymn than (as in *Hymns Ancient and Modern*) an evening hymn.[3] Phrases like 'Swift to its close ebbs out life's little day', 'Hold Thou Thy cross before my closing eyes' (possibly an allusion to the Roman Catholic custom of placing a crucifix in the hands of a dying person, which Lyte would have seen on the Continent[4]), 'Heaven's morning breaks and earth's vain shadows flee' seem to point clearly to the author's approaching death. If the hymn *was* written long before 1847 it must surely have referred to some person dying at the time.

Secondly, there is the line 'When other helpers fail, and comforts flee'. In view of F. A. Jones' account of Lyte's choir members being sent copies

---

[1] *Western Morning News,* 16.9.1947.
[2] *The Times,* 19.11.1947.
[3] e.g. J. Ellerton, *Church Hymns,* folio edition, 1881, as quoted in J. Julian, *Dictionary of Hymnology,* Revised edition, 1907, p. 7.
[4] W. Maxwell-Lyte, *British Weekly,* 3.4.47.

of 'Abide with Me' after they had deserted to the Plymouth Brethren in 1846, there must be a high probability that the words refer to these circumstances. If this argument is accepted it means that the hymn was not written until after 1846.

Another point to notice is that Lyte nearly always copied his poems and hymns into manuscript books, often with the date affixed. According to Walter Maxwell-Lyte's notes, two of Lyte's manuscript notebooks contained 'Abide with Me' but in each case it comes last in the book and there is no trace of any copy existing before 1847.[1] As Maxwell-Lyte comments[2]:

> 'It is almost inconceivable that Lyte could have written a poem of such transcendent beauty without realising that he had composed a masterpiece, and in that case, it would, surely, have appeared among his published works in his lifetime. It is almost equally inconceivable that if the manuscript (*sc.* a manuscript, such as the supposed Le Hunte original, much earlier than 1847) was in existence as late as 1900, when the hymn was well-known, the owner did not realise its value, or that persons now living did not see it.'

The overall evidence, then, is very strongly in favour of Maxwell-Lyte's view that the hymn was not composed in anything like its final form until July or August 1847. It is interesting to speculate how far the hymn may have been *inspired* years before, say by the dying priest voicing 'Abide with me' on his death-bed; this would fit in with John Maxwell-Lyte's suggestion that Lyte started on the hymn while at Marazion. There is no real evidence, however, that this in fact happened.

Until *Hymns Ancient and Modern* was published in 1861, 'Abide with Me' was generally sung to Lyte's own tune. A leaflet with this tune was published by John Wright & Co., Thomas Street, Bristol in 1863 in aid of Brixham's Sunday Schools. It is a dull tune and in 1861 the tune 'Eventide' by Dr W. H. Monk took the public by storm and has largely been used ever since. Dr Monk was Director of Music at King's College, London and Musical Editor of *Hymns Ancient and Modern*, and the story is that shortly before this hymn book was published Dr Monk and the Rev. Sir Henry Baker (Chairman of the Proprietors of Hymns A. & M.) had been discussing a tune for 'Abide with Me'[3]. They considered Lyte's

---

[1] One of these manuscript books, owned by Mr Jack Maxwell-Lyte, son of Walter Maxwell-Lyte, we have seen. The other we have not traced.

[2] W. Maxwell-Lyte, *British Weekly*, 3.4.47.

[3] W. K. Lowther Clarke, *A Hundred Years of Hymns Ancient and Modern*, 1960, pp. 29–30.

tune inadequate and the only alternative was 'Troyte's Chant'. Dr Monk, whose three-year-old daughter had just died,[1] sat down without a piano and wrote out the tune in ten minutes.

Apart from copies of the hymn in Lyte's manuscript books of poems, four different copies in the poet's own handwriting on separate sheets of paper have been described. The first was called by Walter Maxwell-Lyte the 'original' manuscript. It has always been in the possession of the Lyte family and is now owned by Lyte's descendant Mr A. B. Palmes of Chagford, Devon. According to the tradition in the family this was the copy that Lyte handed to his daughter on the afternoon of the Sunday of his last sermon. If this is so we presume that Lyte wrote it before that day, for it seems to be an earlier version than that of the Julia letter. Thus it has 'The darkness thickens' (not 'deepens') in the first verse and 'Speak through the gloom' (instead of 'Shine through the gloom') in the last verse. The text is as follows:

> Abide with me! Fast falls the Eventide;
> The darkness thickens. Lord, with me abide
> When other helpers fail, and comforts flee,
> Help of the helpless, O abide with me!
>
> Swift to its close ebbs out life's little day;
> Earth's joys grow dim, its glories pass away:
> Change and decay in all around I see.
> O Thou who changest not, abide with me!
>
> Not a brief glance I beg, a passing word;
> But as thou dwellst with thy disciples, Lord,
> Familiar, condescending, patient, free,—
> Come, not to sojourn, but abide with me.
>
> Come not in terrors, as the King of kings;
> But kind and good with healing in Thy wings,
> Tears for all woes, a heart for every plea.
> Come, Friend of sinners and thus bide with me.
>
> Thou on my head in early youth did smile,
> And though rebellious and perverse meanwhile,
> Thou hast not left me, oft as I left Thee.
> On to the close, O Lord, abide with me!

[1] Garland, p. 85. Charles Smyth, *The Guardian*, 21.11.1947 says that Monk's widow has testified that the tune was written in her company out of doors at a time of great sorrow.

I need thy presence every passing hour.
What but thy grace can foil the Tempter's power?
Who like Thyself my guide and stay can be?
Through cloud and sunshine, O, abide with me!

I fear no foe with thee at hand to bless:
Ills have no weight, and tears no bitterness.
Where is death's sting? where grave thy victory?
I triumph still, if Thou abide with me.

Hold then thy cross before my closing eyes;
Speak through the gloom, and point me to the skies.
Heaven's morning breaks, and Earth's vain shadows flee!
In life, in death, O Lord, abide with me!

There is a certain roughness of style about this manuscript, including 'all' altered to 'as' in verse 3, which suggests that it might have been the very first transcript.

The second manuscript, the original of which cannot be found, has been sold for many years at All Saints' Church in lithographed copy. The earliest edition of it which we possess is undated but bears a note saying that it was being sold to raise funds to rebuild the old church, which was evidently then still standing. This would put its date at about 1885. It is clearly in Lyte's handwriting and bears his signature underneath. It is again an early version of the hymn; the wording is identical with that of the 'original' version, except that it has 'then abide with me' instead of 'thus bide with me' in verse 4, line 4, and in verse 6, line 2 it appears to have 'fail' for 'foil' and 'powers' for 'power'.

A third manuscript is mentioned by Walter Maxwell-Lyte in his 1947 *British Weekly* article as containing Lyte's 'final revisions'. It was then owned by John Maxwell-Lyte but we have been unable to discover its present whereabouts. Walter Maxwell-Lyte in his notes states that this version is the same as the 'original' except that it has 'deepens' for 'thickens' in verse 1, line 2 and 'Shine' for 'Speak' in the last verse, line 2. In other words it is the same as the printed version in the *Remains*, page 119, as we should have expected. Possibly this was the manuscript which Lyte sent home from Avignon.

The fourth manuscript version is that contained in the Julia letter. This is a little different from the others. In the first verse it has 'deepens' for 'thickens' as do the later versions. In verse 2, line 1 'Swift to its close' is replaced by 'Swift from my grasp'; in the later versions, however, Lyte returned to the former wording. In verse 4, line 4 it has 'thus bide with me', like the 'original' and most other versions. This verse is omitted altogether from most hymn book versions. In verse 6, line 3 it has the unique reading 'guard and guide' instead of 'guide and stay'. In line 4 of that verse 'O, abide with me' is replaced by 'Lord, abide with me'; this alteration was retained in later versions. In verse 8, line 2, as already mentioned, Lyte first wrote 'Speak through the gloom', but he struck out 'Speak' and replaced it by 'Shine'.

A further alteration is seen in both first and second editions of Lyte's *Miscellaneous Poems* (1868 and 1875) where 'Hold Thou thy cross' replaces 'Hold then thy cross' in the last verse. This does not appear in any of the manuscript versions as far as we know; Walter Maxwell-Lyte in his *British Weekly* article presumed that it was a printer's error. Even so, it has found its way into almost all the hymn book versions.

We lastly mention the two manuscript books of poems, each with 'Abide with Me' on the final page. One of these is owned by Mr Jack Maxwell-Lyte who kindly lent it to us. It is bound in hard boards, and is very much a fair copy of Lyte's poems in his own hand. It has an index and also a list of the poems which had been published in *Poems, Chiefly Religious*. Only six of the poems were never published. Apart from punctuation, the version of 'Abide with Me' in this book is identical with that of the *Remains*.

The other notebook was bought for £76 at a London auction in 1939 by Lady Perry for her husband Lord Perry, Chairman of the English Ford Motor Company.[1] According to Walter Maxwell-Lyte's notes the text of 'Abide with Me' in this book was the same as in the 'original' except that in verse 4 there was the unique rendering 'Come, Friend of sinners, and abide with me'. Its present whereabouts are not known.

There is also among the Lyte family papers a printed copy of the hymn taken from 'the Author's MS. Volume now in the possession of his son Farnham Maxwell-Lyte'. This was an earlier version, with 'thickens' in verse 1 and 'Speak through the gloom' in verse 8, but it had 'Come Friend of sinners and thus bide with me' in verse 4. Where this book is we have not been able to trace.

All editions of *Hymns Ancient and Modern* have the same version of the hymn as that in *Miscellaneous Poems*, with 'Hold Thou thy cross' in the last verse, but verses 3, 4 and 5 are omitted altogether, as in almost all hymn

[1] *Daily Express*, 10.2.1939; *Daily Telegraph*, 4.2.1939.

book versions. The *English Hymnal* has 'O, abide with me' instead of 'Lord, abide with me' in the last line of verse 6 (verse 3 in the hymn book); otherwise it is the same.

What is the secret of 'Abide with Me'? Many condemn the hymn as sentimental and over-emotional. Harper comments, for example, 'It is a beautiful hymn but a thing of tears, depression and hopelessness, that leaves you a good deal worse, and a great deal more self-pitying, than before indulging in it.'[1] Others may frown upon the hymn as a popular ditty which most appeals to a football crowd. Yet 'Abide with Me' has always had its magic. It was the favourite hymn of Kings George V[2] and George VI[3] and was sung at the former's funeral, as indeed at Queen Alexandra's. The hymn was General Gordon's favourite and it inspired Shackleton and his men marooned in the icy wastes of the Antarctic. 'Abide with Me' was heard coming from Nurse Cavell's lips as she courageously faced the firing squad.[4] Kitchener had a 'special affection' for the hymn and it was sung at his Memorial Service at St Paul's.[4]

Sir F. J. Wall, then Secretary of the Football Association, told how the hymn first came to be sung at Wembley in 1927.[5] He was handed the draft programme for final revision. One item was to have been the band playing 'Alexander's Rag-Time Band'. Sir Frederick felt moved by a 'mysterious power' to replace it by 'Abide with Me'. When the singing of the hymn commenced, King George V, who was present at the match, stood and bared his head. So the tradition continued.

Garland's explanation of the hymn's popularity was as follows: 'Millions of personal answers (sent to him in response to the questionnaire he circulated) are summed up in the generalisation that it has grown constantly more apt, more full of meaning, throughout the stormy twentieth century. More and more people have found themselves in circumstances in which it answered their spiritual need. There is perhaps a deep-rooted unspoken conviction in the hearts of ordinary men that indeed "the darkness deepens", that other helpers have failed and other comforts have fled, that change and decay are plainly visible in the material world around, that what is true in the individual emergency is

[1] C. G. Harper, *The South Devon Coast,* 1907, p. 166.
[2] Garland, pp. 76f.
[3] F. O. Salisbury, Foreword to Garland's book.
[4] *The Star,* 10.6.1916 and 12.6.1916.
[5] H. J. Garland, *Sunday Times,* 19.10.1947.

also true of the world's fast-developing international situation: "I triumph still if Thou abide with me".[1]

Walter Maxwell-Lyte praises 'Abide with Me' but makes little attempt to explain its popularity. In his *British Weekly* article he says: 'Abide with Me' will live as long as the English language. It has been translated into many foreign tongues and has comforted millions. It is destined to comfort millions more. It represents the triumph of faith and hope over despair.'

James Douglas writes[2]: 'The secret of "Abide with Me" is its divine simplicity, its inspired truthfulness and sincerity. Every word is a cry from the human heart. Its rhythm is magically right because it follows the passion of the soul in wave after wave.' He quotes Ellerton as saying 'It is almost too intense and personal for ordinary congregational use'. 'But that is its magic', Douglas continues, 'It is the human cry of the human heart in the ecstasy and rapture of holy faith. It melts the hardest mind. It transfigures the simplest intellect. In sorrow and consolation it comforts and consoles. There is not a false note in its music. That is why it is the hymn of hymns'.

To the undoubted element of truth in the above we would add one further consideration. Although it is certainly a hymn of faith, it strikes many people as first and foremost a hymn of *sadness,* a hymn that evokes tears. The tune 'Eventide' contributes much to this; it is one of those tunes like 'Crimond' ('The Lord's my Shepherd') and 'Belmont' ('By cool Siloam's shady rill') which in themselves provoke a feeling of sadness. The words of the hymn are sad enough; the tune greatly enhances the effect. There is something in the make-up of the vast majority of human beings which enjoys the shedding of a tear. At over half the funerals at All Saints' to-day the relatives ask for 'Abide with Me'. This may be partly due to the Brixham connection, but we imagine that at many other churches the position would be the same. Even devoted church families are often reluctant to have Resurrection hymns at a departed relative's funeral; they feel, even if wrongly, perhaps, from a Christian point of view, that something has been lost if they have not had the opportunity to shed a tear. This human longing to be sad, if only now and again, explains, we would submit, a good part of the popularity of the hymn. Furthermore, not only is the hymn enveloped in sadness but it promises ultimate joy and triumph. It appeals more to the old and nostalgic than to the young and forward-looking, but its appeal is irresistible even to-day to a vast number of people.

[1] H. J. Garland, *Sunday Times,* 19.10.1947.
[2] J. Douglas, *Sunday Express,* 20.11.1932.

13

THE FINAL JOURNEY

S OMEWHERE between 24 September and 28 September 1847, as we have seen, Lyte left Brixham for the last time, accompanied by his son, John's wife Emily and their servant Mary Pope. Garland and Appleyard say that a large crowd of parishioners and fishermen lined the streets to see him off; the *Remains,* page lii, states that he left 'in some degree of health'. A diary in Lyte's handwriting covers his movements from Friday, 1 October, on which day he left London for the Continent, until about 20 October, but there is little information on his journey from Brixham to London.

Two letters written by Lyte to his wife from London still survive, but neither is dated. They were obviously written within days of each other, however, and Walter Maxwell-Lyte ascribed them to September 1847. They might just have been written in 1846, but the reference to Emily (see below), who was not married nor as far as we know with the party in 1846, suggests an 1847 date. The first letter said that Lyte had got to London 'more dead than alive' but was feeling better. They had dined en route at the home of Mrs Maxwell at Bath; she had been very kind to them and was 'pleased' with Emily. Lyte was to see Mr Jupp about the will that day and on the following Monday, and they would start for the Continent on Thursday. The second letter noted that Mr Jupp and Mr Hogg would be trustees of the estate.

On 1 October, as his diary records, Lyte and his companions left London for Folkestone. They dined at the Pavilion Hotel in the latter town for two-and-a-half shillings each; it was a good dinner in half French and half English style. They had a stern time at the French Customs House: 'All were driven into a vacant room and penned up there like a flock of sheep, no distinction being made between rich and poor' adds Lyte with evident indignation! After a very rigorous search they were allowed to go to their hotels. Passports were very necessary even in those far-off days. They stayed the night at the Hotel Les Bains at the French port (Boulogne?) which was not named in the diary. As so often they were shamefully overcharged. At 9 a.m. on 2 October they started for Abbeville in their old Continental carriage. Having arrived there, the next morning they put their carriage on the train, and travelled in the carriage on the railroad to Paris. For this they were charged £5, which included three free places; they bought second class tickets for the two maids. The second maid is not named; she may have been a French servant.

At Paris the Customs officers were 'very civil', dispensing with all searching. After some difficulty in finding accommodation they found first-floor rooms at the Hotel Westminster, Rue de la Paix, near the Madeleine. 'I was delighted to quit the carriage for a chair and fireside.' They had to stay at Paris until 7 October because of passport difficulties; had they not approached the English Embassy they would have had to stay a further day. While in Paris Lyte saw Dr Louis (?) three times. He only received a superficial opinion from him, however, partly because of language problems and also because any sounding of the chest 'was impossible owing to the noise of the street'!

While in Paris John Lyte visited a College, and one evening the Vice-Principal, a Roman Catholic priest named M. Shechan, came over and chatted to them for an hour. As usual Lyte soon got on to the subject of Roman Catholic religion. 'The little man (Shechan) assured us that so seriously did he hold Confession that if anyone told him in Confession that he had poisoned the chalice from which he was about to drink he would nevertheless drink the wine without hesitation and die rather than divulge what had been confided to him—I could not help putting my tongue in my cheek on hearing this though I said nothing.' This story shows how, close to death as Lyte then was, he still retained his sense of humour and intense interest in life.

On 7 October they took the mid-day train from Paris to Bourges. Lyte was delighted with Bourges Cathedral, which was one of the finest he had ever entered. They stayed the night at the Hotel Le Boeuf near the Cathedral. Then they continued southwards to Sancoins where they spent the night at a small inn. The next day they dined at Moulins and went on to Varennes, a town which had a reputation for cheating the tourist. Despite this they spent the night at an hotel there as 'I was so much worn and fatigued'. Here they were 'atrociously cheated', eight francs being charged for a fire, for instance. As the hotel keeper was also Postmaster they were forced to pay up to get horses to continue their journey!

By now it was Sunday, 10 October; it is not possible to tell from the diary where the third night after Paris was spent; they may have been two nights at Bourges. At all events they proceeded to La Pallise where they stayed at a comfortable and reasonable house. While here Lyte wrote home, saying that he had scarcely recovered from a cold he caught the day before leaving England. He gives an exquisite description of the countryside, resplendent in its autumn tints, but adds: 'Scenery can be ill enjoyed when it is a labour to fetch one breath after another.' He wrote that John and Emily were making every sacrifice on his account. John himself finished the letter, saying that his father was up one day and down the next: sometimes his condition was 'frightening'.

From La Pallise they reached Roanne on 11 October. There it was decided that the party should split up because Lyte was so poorly. Lyte alone (or possibly with Mary Pope) was to go to St Etienne by rail and then to Vienne by omnibus and to Avignon by steamer, while the others were to continue by carriage and meet him later. Lyte reached St Etienne comfortably, fighting the cold with good coal fires, and on reaching the Rhone valley the following day he found the temperature 4–5° F. higher. He records an interesting conversation he had on the bus to Vienne with an English ironfounder who had worked at St Etienne for twenty-seven years.

Reaching Vienne at three o'clock, presumably on 13 October, Lyte found that the Avignon steamer no longer stopped there. So he had to spend the night at Vienne and take a steamer for Valence the next morning whence he could get another steamer for Avignon. He notes that the Rhone has its own beauty, quite equal to that of the Rhine. There were the fine grotesque hills of Languedoc, backed by the snowy peaks of the more distant Alps. At Valence he stayed with Mme. Vacher, evidently a land-lady he had patronised in previous years, who was 'as obliging as ever' and let him have her best bedroom. After tea he found to his dismay that the only steamer to Avignon left at 5 a.m. the next day. So he rose at 4 a.m. and had to scramble over cables, puddles and coal-heaps in the dark, boarding three different steamers before finding himself on the right one!

The steamer scrubbed the bottom of the river all the way down but happily did not stick fast, and in about six hours the Pope's old palace began to show majestically on the sky-line. At Avignon he was received with great warmth by M. and Mme. Pierrou, innkeepers whom again he must have patronised in previous years.

While exact dates are missing from the diary, we presume that Lyte stayed at Avignon for several days from about 15 October. He wrote two letters home on 19 and 20 October, extracts of which are quoted in

the *Remains,* pages cviii and cx. Every evening the Pierrous, or one of
them, chatted with him for an hour in his room in their broken English:
'Their kindness was unbounded and I felt more at home with them than
anywhere since I left dear old Berryhead.' Lyte strolled around the town
alone and searched all the old bookshops; he found little except a MS.
Psalterium in folio, and a Parisian Breviary, both of which he bought.
On 18 October John and Emily had rejoined him, with a tale of woe
about the carriage having broken down between Roanne and Lyons. A
rascal who offered to repair it for 150 francs put in old parts worse than
those he removed, and at Avignon they had to have it all done again, at
about the same cost. John had met a gentleman at Lyons who possessed
170 old manuscripts, including the first part of Livy's works, which he
valued at £100. Lyte thought from the description that the second part
must be at Rome.

With John's help Lyte visited the Public Library at Avignon, which
contained an immense collection of books gathered from all the sup-
pressed convents of the place, though more than half were duplicates.
Lyte took Emily to see Pope John XXII's tomb: 'a beautiful specimen of
florid Gothic.' The Cathedral had little else in it to admire, but Lyte was
somewhat fascinated by the series of apartments in the Pope's Palace 'all
intended for imprisonment or torture of one kind and another'.

In the meantime John had been to Carpentras and his report was so
good that they all decided to go over there. They got horses and reached
the town in two hours: 'They had never before had an English family
there.' The town was clean, the sky clear and the mountains not far away.
The air was 'mild, yet dry and elastic' and they all felt better for their
visit. The town had a very choice library given by its munificent Bishop,
who also built the Hospital and the Town Hall. The library contained
over 12,000 books,including 700 manuscripts; Lyte was very interested
in a 1494 Sarum Missal and a splendid Missale Romanum folio, printed
in Venice about 1500. They returned to Avignon passing fields almost all
planted with madder; M. Pierrou told Lyte it was five times as valuable
as a crop of wheat.

The Lytes set off for Pont de Gard at 2.30 'the same afternoon'—the
date is uncertain. After a very rough journey they arrived at the Pont de
Gard, spending some time gazing at its majestic arches by moonlight.
They went on to Nisines and arrived at the Hotel de Luxembourg a
little after nine o'clock.

Here, sadly, the diary ends, with blank pages following. One more letter survives, commenced at Arles and finished at Aix on 3 November. Part of this is quoted in the *Remains,* page cxii; our extract is from the original letter. Lyte gives a good description of the district and adds: 'On Thursday (i.e. 5 November) we hope to be at Nice and remain there at least a week . . . I have been wonderfully well for the last 10 days . . . Pope has been very poorly . . . last night I feared she would have a fever. We have been obliged to stop here a day to get her better. She is so this morning, but still in bed. I trust however that we shall reach Nice on Friday evening. We shall, I trust, after about a week's rest (there) move on to Genoa and there, if the weather invites, proceed (perhaps by sea) to Leghorn. We shall scarcely be at Rome before the close of the month— I should myself like to go on to Sicily but I fear our money will not last out so far, and then Emily may scarcely be in a stage to encounter a sea voyage.'[1] Lyte trusted 'that the same merciful Father is protecting you who is protecting us', his faith remaining firm to the end.

We take up the last part of the story from the *Remains,* pages lii–lv. 'Within a few hours' journey of Nice, he was seized with influenza, which, soon after his arrival there changed to dysentery, accompanied with very alarming symptoms.' Lyte asked that no medicine be given him which would dim his faculties. He valued the counsel and ministrations of an Anglican clergyman 'whose gentle, yet searching tone, peculiarly fitted him to be a chosen comforter in the hours of trial and pain. From his hands he received, for the last time, the Sacrament of the Lord's Supper, and it seemed as though, in the reception of that most precious Sacrament, all doubt, all disquiet, passed away—he tasted of "that peace which passeth all understanding" '. The priest who attended Lyte was H. E. Manning, then Archdeacon of Chichester but later to become Cardinal Archbishop of Westminster.[2] Lyte had known Manning for years, both through his Oxford Movement connections and because Manning and Samuel Wilberforce had married two sisters of the Sargent family of Lavington.

Lyte was given powerful opiates, the *Remains* tells us, over the first few days of his illness. He was fearful of their stupefying influence but his mind never wandered. He lingered on for days, his patience and cheerfulness never forsaking him. 'His whole soul seemed so imbued with peace and hope, that the last agony and the darkness of the grave dwelt not in his thoughts. One day, on waking from sleep, he said to his faithful attendant: "Oh! there is nothing terrible in death; Jesus Christ steps down

[1] Emily's son, later to become Sir Henry Maxwell-Lyte, was born on 29.5.1848.
[2] S. R. Hole, *The Memories of Dean Hole,* 1892, p. 77.

into the grave before me." And in his case there was nothing terrible; no agony at the last. His prayer was heard, and when his summons came, without a sigh or struggle, he literally fell asleep in Jesus.'

Lyte died at the Hotel de la Pension Anglaise, Nice on 20 November 1847. John Lyte sent a letter home from Nice describing his father's death but this appears to have been lost. Lyte was buried in the middle of the old cemetery at Nice, which is in the grounds of the Church of England Chapel. A plain marble cross marks his grave. In his *British Weekly* article Walter Maxwell-Lyte wrote: 'Tall cypresses, palm trees and olives cast dark shadows over the poet's grave. Nearby the fragrant mimosa waves its golden blossoms, and the blue Mediterranean, the mighty ocean which Lyte loved to extol in verse, laps gently.'

Garland, page 53, states that when news of Lyte's death reached Brixham, J. R. Hogg, now curate-in-charge and soon to be Vicar of All Saints', was asked to hold a Memorial Service at which 'Abide with Me' was sung. From that day onward it began to be sung frequently in Brixham, and gradually it became known all over the land, especially after the publication of *Hymns Ancient and Modern* in 1861.

LYTE'S *THE SPIRIT OF THE PSALMS*—AND
AN ASSESSMENT OF HIS LIFE AND WORK

WHILE space will not allow of a full treatment of *The Spirit of the Psalms,* some comment at least is needed on a work which gave the world such great hymns as 'Praise, my soul, the King of Heaven', 'God of mercy, God of grace' and 'Pleasant are Thy courts above'.

Though great hymns had been written in ancient times and Luther had written some fine hymns for Germany, singing at Church of England services after the Reformation, even up to Lyte's time, was largely limited to the canticles and metrical psalms. The Nonconformists, led by Watts and Doddridge, were singing many hymns by the early nineteenth century, yet the Church of England for the most part clung to Calvin's tradition that only the inspired words of Scripture should be sung in church services. In Queen Mary's reign the leading English Reformers had fled to Switzerland and had been greatly influenced by Calvin, and this had been the result. Hymns such as we love singing to-day, such as Watts' 'When I survey the wondrous Cross', were condemned by many Anglicans in Lyte's time as being no more than the work of man.[1]

In 1562 Sternhold and Hopkins published the final form of their *Whole Book of Psalms,* i.e. metrical psalms or hymns based on the Psalms. These were the only hymns normally allowed to be sung at Church of England services, and this book, later known as the Old Version, met the demand for church music at the time. It could be bound up with the Prayer Book, or Bible, and came to be looked on as a document of the faith. It was at this stage that the custom came in of having hymns (in this case, metrical psalms) as an optional addition to the service instead of, as with the old Office Hymns, a prescribed part of the service itself. The Old Version held the field for generations and continued to be used in some quarters well into the nineteenth century. It aimed to keep very close to the words of Holy Scripture, but this was at the cost of the poetry which was often very poor. An exception to this was Psalm 100, 'All

[1] W. K. Lowther Clarke, *A Hundred Years of Hymns Ancient and Modern,* 1960, pp. 11–12.

people that on earth do dwell', which has lived on to this day. The tunes, however, were good and many are still in use.[1]

In 1696 the New Version was published by Nicholas Brady and Nahum Tate, after there had been growing discontent with the Old. It was authorised by William III in that year as an official alternative. Some of the hymns of the New Version, such as Psalm 34, 'Through all the changing scenes of life', and Psalm 42, 'As pants the hart for cooling streams', were attractive and are still in use. Most of them were dull and spiritless, however, so that not only were many other books of metrical psalms written, but non-scriptural hymns became increasingly popular towards 1800 and were used by unruly Anglicans like the Wesleys as well as by Nonconformists. According to Julian,[2] Lyte's *The Spirit of the Psalms* was actually the 238th partial or complete English metrical psalter to have been written!

The Spirit of the Psalms differed from most of its competitors in the very wide freedom of interpretation Lyte allowed himself; only occasionally did he make any attempt to keep close to the biblical text. In the Preface[3] he states that he has endeavoured 'to condense the leading sentiments of each (psalm) into a few verses for congregational singing. The modern practice of using only three or four verses at a time would render the great majority of the Psalms, if literally translated, unfit, on the score of length, for public worship . . . The author has therefore simply endeavoured to give the *Spirit of each Psalm* in such a compass as the public taste would tolerate'. Lyte adds that Christian metrical psalms ought to be made to express 'all that David himself would have expressed, had he lived under the superior light that we enjoy . . . What therefore he darkly intimates respecting Christ and His Gospel (and the Psalms are full of such intimations) the author has in many instances endeavoured to unfold and expand'. Charmingly he concludes that the writing of the book 'has sweetly filled up the intervals of laborious ministerial duty, and solaced many of the human trials to which human life is ever subject. Conversing with the divine Psalmist in his beautiful and spiritual compositions, he hopes that he has learned more of himself and more of God; and been enabled sometimes to lift his heart in humble union with the Sweet Singer of Israel'.[4]

[1] W. K. Lowther Clarke, *op. cit.,* p. 12.
[2] J. Julian, *Dictionary of Hymnology,* Revised edition, 1907, p. 930.
[3] H. F. Lyte, *The Spirit of the Psalms,* 2nd edition, 1834, pp. iii–iv.
[4] H. F. Lyte, *op. cit.,* p. vii.

The book contains at least one version, usually two or three, of each of the 150 Psalms. Not all the versions are Lyte's own, however, for he also included 'the best and most popular passages of the ordinary New Version of our Church'.[1] The latter, which included such favourites as 'Through all the changing scenes of life', were marked with asterisks to distinguish them from Lyte's own compositions. Even the New Version psalms, however, were in many cases modified by Lyte. The book continued 320 metrical psalms in all, of which 270 were Lyte's original compositions. No doubt this substantial work was written over a number of years. Some of the hymns would have been composed during the leisurely spells at Sway and Dittisham, when so many of his poems were written. Many of his hymns and metrical psalms were undoubtedly written for his congregation at All Saints', however, where he had already ministered for ten years when the book appeared. Lyte's own account of the changed nature of his poems on the Psalms after he came to Brixham (see above, page 20) indicates that many were written while he was at All Saints'. F. A. Jones[2] states that 'God of mercy, God of grace' (Psalm 67, 2nd version) was 'one of Mr Lyte's earliest hymns and was written, not at Berry Head . . . but at Burton House (Brixham)'.

Lyte was by no means the first to attempt liberal interpretations of the psalms. Watts had done much the same in hymns such as 'O God, our help in ages past', based on Psalm 90 and published in 1719, as Montgomery later did with 'Hail to the Lord's Anointed' (Psalm 72, 1821). Indeed a somewhat old-fashioned critic went as far as to write that Watts was by no means the originator of 'the questionable practice of rendering the Psalms not literally but interpretively'.[3] It is probable, however, that few if any have surpassed Lyte as regards the extent and poetical quality of his collection. The Preface is dated January 1834; the second edition, of which we were lent a copy, appeared the same year. An attractive volume for its day, it is of the size of a small prayer book with 221 pages and an index.

As examples of the poet's 'christianising' of a psalm we take first the opening verse of Psalm 22 (2nd version):

O what a conquest Jesus won,
  When on the fatal tree
He felt his destined labour done,
  And earth from guilt set free!

[1] *ibid.*, p. v.
[2] F. A. Jones, *Famous Hymns and their Authors,* 3rd edition, 1905, p. 212.
[3] J. Holland, *The Psalmists of Britain,* 1843, Vol. 2, p. 146.

All five verses of this version are centred on Jesus, whereas Lyte's third version of the same psalm does not mention Christ at all. Secondly, the opening verse of Psalm 40 (2nd version) is of interest:

> 'I come, I come', the Saviour cries,
>   'The wrath of God to brave',
> My sinful soul, awake, arise,
>   And fly to Christ to save.

The four verses of this version all concern Christ and his atoning Cross, and in verse 3 'O Lamb of God' is used.

The limit of Lyte's paraphrasing is almost certainly reached in the first version of Psalm 48. The first and last verses read:

> Great is the Lord; his praise be great!
>   Ye lands, your tributes bring.
> And, Britain, thou, his chosen seed
>   Be first to praise thy King.

> But, Lord, be Britain still thy choice;
>   Still walk around her towers.
> Still let her sons in thee rejoice,
>   And cry 'the Lord is ours!'

The most famous of Lyte's metrical psalms is 'Praise, my soul, the King of Heaven' (E.H. 470, A & M Revised 365) which is the second of his three versions of Psalm 103. From the standpoint of church worship we would claim that this is one of the greatest hymns that the Anglican Church has produced. In keeping with the 'Catholic' tone of the first edition of *Hymns Ancient and Modern* the hymn has a Godward orientation; although human beings are mentioned there is no preoccupation with the individual worshipper. Its brevity compared with many Free Church hymns is thoroughly Anglican. Straightforward and uncomplicated it is full of joy, thanksgiving and praise. Its high quality as a poem is capped by Goss' magnificent tune which first appeared in Brown-Borthwick's 1869 *Supplemental Hymn and Tune Book,* 3rd edition. In Lyte's time it had been sung to the eighteenth-century tune 'Alleluia dulce carmen'. As usual the *English Hymnal* follows Lyte exactly, apart from minor differences of punctuation, but it omits the fourth of the original five verses, which was as follows:

> Frail as summer's flowers we flourish;
>   Blow the wind, and it is gone.
> But while mortals rise and perish,
>   God endures unchanging **on.**
> Praise him! Praise him!
>   Praise the high eternal One!

Some interesting changes in the text were made in the Standard Edition of *Hymns Ancient and Modern*. For instance Lyte's 'Angels help us to adore him' in the last verse was altered to 'Angels in the height, adore Him', presumably because the invocation of angels was then unfashionable in the Church of England. In the same verse Lyte's 'Sun and moon, bow down before him' was modified to 'Saints triumphant, bow before Him', we imagine because the mention of sun and moon in such a context was thought to savour of idolatry. In either case Lyte's version is the larger-minded, and the editors of the Revised edition of *Hymns Ancient and Modern* were wise to return to the original wording. In both editions of this book the words 'Praise him! praise him!' are changed to 'Alleluia! Alleluia!'

'God of mercy, God of grace' (E.H. 395, A & M Revised 264) was the second of three versions of Psalm 67. The *English Hymnal* follows Lyte's text exactly, apart from punctuation. The only change made by *Hymns Ancient and Modern,* both editions, is in verse 2, line 5, which is 'At thy feet their *tribute* pay', whereas Lyte and *English Hymnal* have 'tributes'. Henry Smart's nineteenth-century tune 'Heathlands' was originally set to this hymn, which it suits admirably and is still the normal tune to-day. This is one of Lyte's metrical psalms which keeps fairly close, in its thought if not in the letter, to the Scriptural text. Though usually classed as a General hymn it is often regarded as a missionary hymn, from such words as:

> Fill thy church with light divine;
> And thy saving health extend
> Unto earth's remotest end.

Another of Lyte's versions which has become well known is 'Pleasant are thy courts above'; it is Lyte's paraphrase of 'O how amiable are thy dwellings: thou Lord of hosts!' (Psalm 84). It is the second of the three versions of this Psalm (E.H. 469, A & M Revised 240) and both these hymn books keep almost exactly to Lyte's words. A delightfully happy hymn, it is sung to several tunes, being set to W. B. Gilbert's tune 'Maidstone' in the first edition of *Hymns Ancient and Modern,* but now often sung to J. Hintze's seventeenth-century tune 'Salzburg', a bright and joyful melody which exactly suits the tenor of the words.

Two more of Lyte's metrical psalms which, though popular in their day, were omitted from the Revised edition of *Hymns Ancient and Modern* (and also from the *English Hymnal*) are 'Praise the Lord, his glories show' (Psalm 150, Hymns A & M Standard 544) and 'Far from my heav'nly home' (Psalm 137: 'By the waters of Babylon we sat down and wept', Hymns A & M Standard 284). In the first of these Lyte's words are joyful and splendid, but there are only two verses and the two tunes, though written by such able composers as Sir John Goss and the Rev. Sir F. A. G. Ouseley, are both unexciting. 'Far from my heav'nly home', like the psalm itself is sad, but looks forward in faith to future life in the 'Saints' abode'. It has only four verses, however, and the tune, actually called 'Lyte' and composed by J. Wilkes shortly before 1861, is dreary in the extreme. Both these hymns are now largely forgotten.

Let us now consider some contemporary and later criticism of *The Spirit of the Psalms*. Holland in 1843 remarked that it would be impossible to express the 'spirit' of the Psalmist in 'five or six quatrains of English rhyme . . . the book does, in fact, consist of *Hymns*, composed, in a certain sense, in "The Spirit of the Psalms": but on the whole no more calculated to give any idea of the entire meaning of "The Book of Psalms", than would a series of "Imitations", of the Odes and Epistles of Horace, in which the original names and incidents were dropped, and English sentiments and associations substituted for those of the genuine text, give the reader any notion of the productions of the Latin poet . . . As a whole, then, Mr Lyte's work must chiefly be indebted for its legitimate praise, to the degree in which it approaches the hitherto unsurpassed merit of the Psalmody of Dr Watts'. On the other hand Holland feels that Lyte's work completely lacks that 'compact concatenation of thought and expression, which must so generally strike a pious reader on a first acquaintance with Watts'.[1]

Josiah Miller, writing in 1869, comments: 'Lyte's hymns are free from harshness, correct in their versification, and always full of Scriptural thought and spiritual meaning. Some of them are of a high order.'[2]

Julian comments: 'Though it touches the whole psalter, and though there are a few among the best that have a joyous tone, such as the sunny rendering of Ps. 84 "Pleasant are thy courts above"; still it is with the tenderness and tearfulness of the Psalms that he is most deeply penetrated . . . Ps. 55 "O that I had, my Saviour, the wings of a dove", a successful treatment of an undignified metre, illustrates his habit of isolating the sad part of a psalm.'[3]

[1] J. Holland, *The Psalmists of Britain,* 1843, Vol. 2, pp. 344–6.
[2] J. Miller, *Singers and Songs of the Church,* 1869, p. 433.
[3] J. Julian, *op. cit.,* p. 921.

We would differ a little from the last critic over the sadness of Lyte's metrical psalms. Lyte certainly had a tender nature; his life was one of much sadness and he had a deep understanding of sadness. Several of his poems are on the subject of people dying. In his later years Lyte showed markedly the *spes phthisica,* a characteristic 'sunshine through the clouds' attitude to life which is seen in most advanced tuberculosis patients and which comes out very plainly in the hymn 'Abide with Me'. Lyte's metrical psalter is full of happy verses, however, such that it is rarely possible to turn over two pages without finding some verses radiant with joy. Indeed all the hymns we have so far mentioned, with the sole exceptions of 'Abide with Me' and 'Far from my heavenly home', are joyful in their tone.

For years *The Spirit of the Psalms* was widely used in Anglican churches, as Lyte's Obituary notice testifies.[1] When, with the publication of *Hymns Ancient and Modern* in 1861, the prejudice against non-scriptural hymns was finally done away, the need for metrical psalters in the Church of England no longer existed. There was a return to Prayer Book psalms and Lyte's book naturally faded into the background. But it remains a very worthy contribution to Psalmody, the more remarkable achievement in that it was written in the middle of an immensely busy pastoral life.

Our last quotations are from a modern critic, Erik Routley, which provided a suitable note on which to conclude. 'Watts's zeal for reformation and impatience of the outdated carried him to points well beyond the bounds of absurdity; but he opened the way for the magnificent psalm-hymns of Montgomery and Lyte', comments Routley with just appreciation of Lyte's poetic gift.[2] Later in the same book, however, Routley adds: 'Lyte was an obscure country curate who has no claim to fame beyond his saintly character and a handful of hymns. But 'Abide with Me' ranks with the classics in every sense, and it has successfully stood up to harder working than perhaps any hymn in the language.'[3]

Allowing that 'an obscure country curate' is scarcely a fair description of Lyte and perhaps reflects the fact that no adequate *Life* of him has hitherto been published, how was it possible that a man with such a wealth of talent, and with a fair number of influential friends, could ever come thus to be described? Despite his poetic gifts, his scholarship,

[1] *Exeter Flying Post,* 2.12.1847. The Obituary describes Lyte's metrical psalm as presenting 'a rare union of elegant poetry and devotional feeling'.
[2] E. Routley, *Hymns and Human Life,* 1952, p. 15.
[3] *ibid.,* p. 84.

his great wit and personal charm, his assiduous pastoral labours and brilliance of oratory, Lyte was never even appointed a Prebendary of his Cathedral (as was the far less talented Vicar of Brixham, Robert Holdsworth), let alone offered the senior post which his abilities would seem to have merited. How could this be? Part of the answer, especially in his later years, may have been his ill-health. Even as early as his Geneva journey (1827) Lyte was suffering from severe pain and 'fainting fits'. The other reason, we would suggest, was purely and simply his saintly lack of desire for self-advancement. Such influential friends as George Canning and William and Samuel Wilberforce, as we have seen, wished Lyte to keep in close touch with them. Partly through self-effacement, however, and partly through sheer preoccupation with his busy pastoral duties, he allowed these contacts to lapse. It may not be strictly true that he refused all preferment but it is clear that, whatever may have been his reasons for seeking the Crediton post, for many years he was perfectly happy to regard his charge at Brixham, despite the hard work, poor pay and other drawbacks, as the sphere of work to which God had called him.

Justice came to Lyte's reputation, as it did to Teilhard de Chardin's, after his death. Within a few years of the appearance of *Hymns Ancient and Modern* in 1861, 'Abide with Me' had become nationally famous. Nowadays this hymn and 'Praise, my soul, the King of Heaven' are known all over the world. Between 1886 and 1907 the splendid new All Saints' Church was built at Brixham in his memory. The crowning glory came in the centenary year of his death, 1947, when an alabaster tablet bearing the simple inscription:

Henry Francis Lyte

1793–1847

"Abide with Me, Fast Falls the Eventide"

was fixed in Westminster Abbey, being placed appropriately just below the bust of the great hymn-writer Dr Isaac Watts, and close to the memorial tablet to John and Charles Wesley. Lyte had come into his own, and his great work still goes on wherever his hymns are sung.

A SHORT SELECTION OF LYTE'S POEMS

A SHORT SELECTION OF LYTE'S POEMS

Four Poems from *Poems, Chiefly Religious*

ON DREAMING OF MY MOTHER

Stay, gentle shadow of my mother, stay:
  Thy form but seldom comes to bless my sleep,
Ye faithless slumbers, flit not thus away,
  And leave my wistful eyes to wake and weep.
Oh! I was dreaming of those golden days
  When, will my guide, and pleasure all my aim,
I rambled wild through childhood's flowery maze,
  And knew of sorrow scarcely by her name.
Those scenes are fled! and thou, alas, art fled,
  Light of my heart and guardian of my youth!
Then come no more to slumbering fancy's bed,
  To aggravate the pangs of waking truth:
Or, if kind sleep these visions will restore,
  Oh, let me sleep again, and never waken more!

AGNES

I saw her in childhood—
  A bright gentle thing,
Like the dawn of the morn,
  Or the dews of the spring:
The daisies and harebells
  Her playmates all day;
Herself as light-hearted
  And artless as they.

I saw her again—
  A fair girl of eighteen,
Fresh glittering with graces
  Of mind and mien.
Her speech was all music;
  Like moonlight she shone;
The envy of many,
  The glory of one.

Years, years fleeted over—
   I stood at her foot:
The bud had grown blossom,
   The blossom was fruit.
A dignified mother,
   Her infant she bore;
And looked, I thought, fairer
   Than ever before.

I saw her once more—
   'Twas the day that she died:
Heaven's light was around her,
   And God at her side;
No wants to distress her,
   No fears to appal—
O then, I felt, then,
   She was fairest of all!

ON A NAVAL OFFICER BURIED IN THE ATLANTIC
(later set to music by Sir Arthur Sullivan)

There is, in the wide, lone sea,
   A spot unmarked, but holy;
For there the gallant and the free
   In his ocean bed lies lowly.

Down, down, within the deep,
   That oft to triumph bore him,
He sleeps a sound and pleasant sleep,
   With the salt waves washing o'er him.

He sleeps serene, and safe
   From tempest or from billow,
Where the storms, that high above him chafe
   Scarce rock his peaceful pillow.

The sea and him in death
   They did not dare to sever:
It was his home while he had breath;
   'Tis now his rest for ever.

Sleep on, thou mighty dead!
   A glorious tomb they've found thee—
The broad blue sky above thee spread,
   The boundless waters round thee.

No vulgar foot treads here;
No hand profane shall move thee;
But gallant fleets shall proudly steer,
And warriors shout, above thee.

And when the last trump shall sound,
And tombs are asunder riven,
Like the morning sun from the wave thou'lt bound,
To rise and shine in heaven.

SPARE MY FLOWER

O spare my flower, my gentle flower,
The slender creature of a day!
Let it bloom out its little hour,
And pass away.
Too soon its fleeting charms must lie
Decayed, unnoticed, overthrown.
O hasten not its destiny,—
Too like thy own.

The breeze will roam this way to-morrow,
And sigh to find his playmate gone:
The bee will come its sweets to borrow,
And meet with none.
O spare! and let it still outspread
Its beauties to the passing eye,
And look up from its lowly bed
Upon the sky.

O spare my flower! Thou know'st not what
Thy undiscerning hand would tear:
A thousand charms thou notest not
Lie treasured there.
Not Solomon, in all his state,
Was clad like nature's simplest child;
Nor could the world combined create
One floweret wild.

Spare then this humble monument
Of an Almighty's power and skill;
And let it at His shrine present
Its homage still.
He made it who makes nought in vain:
He watches it who watches thee;
And he can best its date ordain
Who bade it be.

O spare my flower—for it is frail;
  A timid, weak, imploring thing—
And let it still upon the gale
      Its moral fling.
That moral thy reward shall be:
  Catch the suggestion, and apply:—
'Go, live like me', it cries; 'like me
      'Soon, soon to die'.

A few of Lyte's unpublished poems

ON MY NATIVE LAND
(1814)

Beloved Scotland, how shall I forbear,
To cast a fond but heavy look to thee.
When shall be mine the soldier's lot to share
My native hills and home again to see?
O loveliest land of all the world to me,
Theme of my sleeping and my waking dreams,
Dim not my eyes, ye tears of ecstasy;
How bright thy distant scene to memory seems.

Ye hills of Cheviot, where my infant feet
Have rambled wild through many a summer day;
Ye banks of Tweed, where once I thought it sweet
To lie and listen to the skylark's lay.
A sad farewell. I still had hoped to stray
And find within your bowers a refuge yet.
The dream is fled, but in this form of clay
Till every spark of feeling shall be set;
Land of my birth, this heart shall never thee forget.

A WISH
(1813)

Had I the power which men of yore
From gracious fairies oft possessed,
To chuse my home and round it pour
    The joys I deemed the best
No costly palace would I claim;
I would not sigh for wealth or fame.

But in some wild romantic spot
Where woodlands waved and waters ran,
I'd build my woodbine clustered cot
    Afar from busy man.
There flowers should bloom and birds should sing
And hares and fawns around me spring.

Behind a garden duly stored
A lawn with sheep before my door;
Enough to crown my frugal board
    And something for the poor.
With a few books of various kind
To stir the heart and store the mind.

A wife with smiles should light my home,
Four cherubs prattle round their sire
And now and then a friend should come
    To cheer our evening fire.
Then all to bed when prayers were done
To rise at morning with the sun.

And thus I'd steal through many a year
In health, contentment, peace and love,
Esteemed by all around me here
    And God my friend above;
Till death in mildest form should come
And bear me to a better home.

'WHAT SHALL I DO?'

Oppressed by sin, oppressed by shame,
By crimes I cannot count or name.
Cast off by all and nigh despair,
Where shall I turn? O tell me where.

If to the giddy world I go
Its heartless crowd but mocks my woe,
Its worthless toys no more can please
Or cheat me into transient ease.

If back to sin I rush amain,
T'is but to deepen every pain.
The guilty madness soon is o'er
And conscience fiercer than before.

No spot on earth can hide my head;
The very grave gives up its dead.
Without a friend, a plea, a prayer,
Where shall I turn? O tell me where.

Where should I turn but, Lord, to Thee?
Thy mercy still is large and free.
'Come back', it cries. Nay grace divine
Can pardon guilt e'en black as thine.

Lord, lead me humbled to Thy feet;
O make conversion's work complete.
My sinful soul renew, restore,
And build me up to fall no more.

'COME, LORD JESUS!'

O give me back my hopes again,
    O give me back my peace.
Take what Thou wilt. I'll not complain,
    But spare, O spare me these.

I care not what the toil may be;
    I care not what the cost.
Cheap are the joys that spring from Thee,
    Though all for them be lost.

I ask not pomp, I ask not fame,
    I ask not worldly store;
One smile of Thine is all I claim,
    I want, I wish no more.

Whate'er it be that from my soul
    Thy presence, Lord, may chase,
How freely now I yield the whole
    So Thou wilt take its place.

Without Thee joys are nothing worth
    And ills no ills with Thee;
Thy smile is Heaven begun on earth,
    Thy frown a Hell to me.